D0712649

DISCARD

THE RITUAL THEORY OF MYTH

The Ritual Theory of Myth

JOSEPH FONTENROSE

UNIVERSITY OF CALIFORNIA PRESS

BERKELEY, LOS ANGELES, LONDON

1971

UNIVERSITY OF CALIFORNIA PUBLICATIONS
FOLKLORE STUDIES: 18

UNIVERSITY OF CALIFORNIA PRESS
BERKELEY AND LOS ANGELES
CALIFORNIA

◇

UNIVERSITY OF CALIFORNIA PRESS, LTD.
LONDON, ENGLAND

ISBN: 0-520-01924-5
© 1966 BY THE REGENTS OF THE UNIVERSITY OF CALIFORNIA
CALIFORNIA LIBRARY REPRINT SERIES EDITION 1971
PRINTED IN THE UNITED STATES OF AMERICA

PREFACE

MYTH has a great vogue today, and nowhere so much as in literary criticism. Some critics are finding myth everywhere, especially those who follow the banner of the "myth-ritual" school—or perhaps I should say banners of schools, since ritualists do not form a single school or follow a single doctrine. But most of them are agreed that all myths are derived from rituals and that they were in origin the spoken part of a ritual performance. Ultimately all ritualists come to rest under the shadow of the Golden Bough. So in this study I examine not only the doctrines of Lord Raglan, Stanley Hyman, and other conspicuous ritualists, but also (both literally and figuratively) the tree under which they stand. I investigate the bough itself and the strange priest who allegedly guarded it; I investigate the Frazerian royal victim, whose unhappy fate affects us still in manifold ways—if the ritualists are right.

The ritual interpretation of myth is by no means confined to literary criticism. It has a wide influence in many fields, although few anthropologists, folklorists, or classicists accept it, despite ritualist assertions to the contrary. Yet classical scholars and anthropologists had much to do with the building of the ritualist interpretations: Frazer himself was both classicist and anthropologist; Jane Harrison, who is Hyman's main scholarly support, was a classical scholar much influenced by the findings of anthropology (and this statement is equally true of her close friends, Gilbert Murray and Francis Cornford). The writings of Frazer and Harrison have affected so many fields of study and have influenced so many readers that they deserve the attention that I give them here.

I wish to thank Professors William Bascom and Louis MacKay for reading portions of early drafts and for their comments and criticisms, from which I have benefited; Edwin Loeb for a copy of his *In Feudal Africa,* for references to books and articles, and for information drawn from his own knowledge of African peoples; William N. Fenton of the New York State Museum and Science Service for information on Iroquois rites and myths; all friends who have taken an interest in my study of the myth-ritual relationship and who have made suggestions; finally, Miss Lynda Spence of the Editorial Department of the University of California Press for careful editorial work and attention to details of style.

J. F.

CONTENTS

PROLOGUE

In 1921, writing an introduction to his edition and translation of Apollodoros' *Library*, Sir James George Frazer was content to define myths as "mistaken explanations of phenomena, whether of human life or of external nature." This is the definition of myth which prevailed in the nineteenth century: men saw in myth a product of man's supposedly innate intellectual curiosity about the world around him; myth, they said, was a kind of primitive scientific theory. This view of myth still has adherents, although most mythologists and folklorists now consider it to be too intellectualistic. Indeed, Frazer's definition was already old-fashioned in 1921, and another theory of myth had won attention and considerable favor— a theory largely derived from Frazer's own *Golden Bough*, first published in 1890. This was the ritual theory of myth origins, derived initially from Robertson Smith and Frazer, and promoted in the earlier years of this century by Arnold van Gennep, author of *Rites de passage*, and by the so-called Cambridge school— Jane Harrison, Gilbert Murray, Francis Cornford, A. B. Cook. Since 1920 the ritual theory has had a number of champions. Most ardent recently have been Lord Raglan and Stanley Hyman.

Lord Raglan depends mainly upon *The Golden Bough*, accepting the data and primary thesis, but rejecting Frazer's evolutionism, and upon S. H. Hooke's theory of a myth-ritual pattern which prevailed throughout the ancient Near East, and in which the central figure was the divine king. Hyman relies principally upon Frazer and Jane Harrison—her *Themis*, he tells us (1962b:24), changed his life. He is hospitable to all ritual theorists, however inconsistent one's views may be with another's. In three essays he has called the roll of honor: Smith, Frazer, Harrison, Murray, Cornford, Robertson, Weston, Hooke, Hocart, Raglan, Troy, Rourke, Fergusson, and a number of others. He tells us categorically that the ritual theory offers the only sound interpretation of myth: any dissenter is willfully turning his back on the truth and is either naive or, what is worse, a Euhemerist—which no respectable mythologist should want to be.

Raglan and Hyman carry the ritual interpretation to greater extremes than other ritualists do, and they apply it more universally. And so scholars in this field are likely to dismiss them as wild and to esteem them less than the scholars on whom they depend (Frazer, Harrison, Hooke, Hocart); they are in fact derivative and have done little or no primary research of their own. Yet it is the extreme and derivative nature of their views which renders them fit standard-bearers of the ritualist camp, and I have therefore placed them at the center of my critique of the ritual theory of myth origins; they will call on their authorities—Frazer, Harrison and others—when they need them for support. For Raglan and Hyman boldly accept all consequences of the ritualists' position and follow the theory into regions where their more cautious teachers have feared to tread.*

---

* See Hyman 1948 (chap. iv, especially pt. 3), 1949, 1955. In each essay Hyman does about the same thing: he gives an historical sketch of the ritual theory, naming authors and titles, expressing approval of each, and telling us throughout that a ritual theory is the only right view of myth.

For works cited by author's name and year of publication, see the appended Bibliography. I cite Raglan's *The Hero* as *H* and his *The Origins of Religion* as *OR;* and I cite *The Hero* by chapters, which are fairly short, so that the reader may consult either the 1936 edition or the recent paperbound edition, in which the pagination is different.

Although Lord Raglan died in 1964 (after I had written much of this monograph), I refer to him for convenience in the present tense, especially since I often couple his name with Hyman's as joint subjects of verbs.

1

RAGLAN'S ROYAL VICTIM

IF ALL MYTHS have a ritual origin, do all myths arise ultimately from a single ritual, or do all rituals, and only rituals, have a myth-engendering power? The logically simpler alternative is Lord Raglan's choice: all myths are ritual texts and all myth-ritual complexes go back to a single ancient ritual. What about legends and folktales? For they have many of the same themes, patterns, and kinds of character that are found in myth. Lord Raglan sees no real differences among traditional tales: a legend or folktale is simply a myth cut loose from its ritual. As he sees it, all traditional tales, all existing rituals, all religious systems, and, in fact, a good deal else—magic, nursery rhymes, games, riddles, etiquette—are derived from a single Ur-ritual. Historical events, intellectual curiosity, dreams, fantasies, poetic invention, have nothing to do with either the origin or the development of myths, or of any part of them.[1]

SACRIFICE OF THE DIVINE KING

Raglan's is a diffusionist theory of sweeping proportions: it purports to account for the religions and myths of pre-Columbian America as well as for those of the Old World.[2] What was this Ur-ritual which so powerfully stirred men's emotions and imaginations that in manifold forms it still sways men's minds today and has been the sole generator of religions, mythologies, and folklore? It was not the very first ritual in the world: Lord Raglan grants ritual to palaeolithic man, but does not believe that it had any effect on historic and known rituals (OR 51). "The original ritual," says Raglan, "so far as can be judged from the general pattern, was based on the existence of a king who was killed and replaced annually" (H xiii fin.). That is, the original myth-ritual pattern began with the annual sacrifice of a king and the installation of his successor. Raglan describes the evolution of the ritual as follows:

In the first [stage] it was the divine king who was regularly sacrificed; in the second somebody else was regularly sacrificed as a substitute for the divine king; with the progress of civilization came a third stage, in which a human victim was sacrificed in times of emergency, but at other times a pretense was made of killing him, but some other victim was substituted. In the fourth stage the victim was never human, but was usually treated in such a way as to indicate that it once had been. (1955:81)

In some late neolithic kingdom of the ancient Near East men thought it a good idea to kill their "divine king" every year; neighboring kingdoms took up the practice with alacrity, and it spread in ever-widening circles until it embraced the world—to everyone's satisfaction, it seems, except perhaps the divine king's.[3]

---

[1] Raglan 1936, 1949. His books are strange compounds of lucidity and absurdity, as pointed out by Edmund Leach in his review of Raglan's recent The Temple and the House (New York Review of Books, September 16, 1965, pp. 16–17).

[2] Raglan almost ignores the Americas; but three times he adduces Mexican parallels (H xv, xviii, xxi), once quotes Lang on Algonquin and Eskimo folktales (H xii), and once quotes MacCulloch on Algonquin myths (H xv).

[3] Raglan puts the place of origin in the ancient Near East without defining it more exactly (H xiv init., OR 67–68). He seems to lean toward Egypt, since with some reservations he approves Elliot Smith's pan-Egyptian theory (OR 35). He may be further influenced by his own experiences in the Sudan and by the African evidence which he adduces.

And so charged with emotion was this ceremony that it not only colored but provided the whole mythico-religious structure of human society thereafter.

In its first stage, apparently, the ancient ritual had become elaborate and dramatic. According to Raglan it consisted of six acts:

(*a*) A symbolical destruction of the old world by flood and fire.

(*b*) The killing of a sacred victim after a mock combat.

(*c*) The dismemberment of the victim and construction of a "new world" from his members.

(*d*) The making of a pair of human figures from clay and the victim's blood.

(*e*) The coming to life of the images in the persons of a young man and woman who were, or were supposed to be, a brother and sister.

(*f*) A sacred marriage between the pair, who were then regarded as the parents of the newly created race of men. (*OR* 68–69)

What is the evidence for this Ur-ritual? Raglan says, "There is evidence from the myths, and from recorded and existing rites," and it is plain that he has done his best to work in flood myths, combat myths, creation myths, and the sacred-marriage rite. He has in fact derived most of it from S. H. Hooke's festival program, which Hooke considers to be the basic ritual pattern of the ancient Near East:

(*a*) The dramatic representation of the death and resurrection of the god.

(*b*) The recitation or symbolic representation of the myth of creation.

(*c*) The ritual combat, in which the triumph of the god over his enemies was depicted.

(*d*) The sacred marriage.

(*e*) The triumphal procession, in which the king played the part of the god followed by a train of lesser gods or visiting deities.[4]

Here the ritual has obviously reached Raglan's fourth stage of development. Oddly enough Hooke does not mention sacrifice as one of the elements; apparently the sacrifice is part of the first element (*a*). Applying a Frazerian interpretation to Hooke's pattern, Raglan derives his whole first stage from it, except for his first act. Logic suggests an old world destroyed before a new world created, and the flood myths offer Raglan what he needs. The "divine victim developed into the divine king," said Raglan in 1949 (*OR* 73). The first performers of the ritual had no kings as yet: the process is sacrificial victim > king = god (the first kings were not rulers). But in 1955, as we have seen, he said that in the first stage the king was sacrificed, in the second simply a human victim as substitute. Probably this is incomplete statement rather than inconsistency or revision of views. Raglan would diagram the whole process as human victim > divine king > substitute human victim > animal. But now we have the divine king developing out of a human victim (who is not yet a king) and then giving place to a human victim (who is no longer a king). We are back where we started; now, however, the human victim does not become a king, but gives place to an animal. Raglan also does not make evident any link between the powerless divine king and subsequent kings who ruled as absolute monarchs. Why should we call him *king*? If the earliest ruling kings took over a title formerly borne by sacrificed kings, what was the connection?

Raglan's whole structure, we perceive, rests on a single foundation, the annual sacrifice of a divine king or divine victim. What is the evidence for this sacrifice?

---

[4] Hooke 1933:8; see *H* xiv *init.*, *OR* 67; Hocart 1927: 70–71.

Raglan insists that his opponents produce evidence for their views, and we have a right to expect him to be well provided with evidence for his own. He does indeed refer us to the appropriate section of *The Golden Bough* (part III, *The Dying God*), saying that Frazer "abundantly provides [the evidence] that all kings were once put to death at the end of a fixed term" (*OR* 71); and he refers us to the evidence collected by Hooke, Hocart, and their school for the ancient Near Eastern myth-ritual pattern. So in examining Raglan's evidence we are in fact looking at the evidence which Frazer, Hooke, and Hocart have to offer. This evidence falls into two general categories, the historical and the ethnographical.

ANCIENT EVIDENCE FOR KING SACRIFICE

We must deal first with the historical evidence, since if this theory is sound it should have abundant support in surviving literature and art, and Frazer does appear to provide a good deal of evidence. We must look back to the ancient Near East first, to the earliest civilizations, in one of which Raglan and Hooke place the center of diffusion. These lands, especially Egypt, had divine kings (i.e., kings believed to be gods and worshipped as such). But do we find the periodic ritual sacrifice in Egypt or Mesopotamia? Do we find any king-killing at all whether at regular or irregular intervals? On Egyptian kingship, C. N. Deedes, one of Hooke's school, says, "The actual killing of the king-god, . . . remains a mystery in Egyptian history"; the mystery is simply that "No account of it has ever yet been found." There is apparently no mystery about Sumer, where according to Deedes, "there are seals, dating back to about 3000 B.C., on which is depicted the actual killing of the king."[5] Splendid evidence—if the seals are correctly interpreted. However, on consulting Frankfort's *Cylinder Seals,* I found that they represent the sun-god Shamash killing an enemy; it is not a sacrifice, and the enemy is not the king.[6]

In Mesopotamia, as in Egypt, there is no record of an annual or periodic killing of the king. Yet some Mesopotamian kingdoms had the institution of *shar-puhi,* substitute king. When omens indicated that danger threatened the king or the nation, the king made a show of abdicating and of turning over his office to a substitute, who took over the royal insignia and sat upon the throne.[7] The substitution was complete; otherwise it would be ineffective for its purpose. The substitute was really king for the period, except in one important respect; he had to leave the throne as soon as the dangers were declared at an end; he did not dare employ the prerogatives of his office in order to retain them.[8] And the *shar-puhi's*

---

[5] In Hooke 1935:23. See also Moret 1927, who approves Frazer's theory and attempts to find king-killing in ancient Egypt. Like Frazer and Raglan, he can point only to the Osiris myth, the legend of King Bocchoris burned alive, the custom at Meroe (Diod. 3.5–7, on which see p. 10 below), and the ritual of the Sed festival; see Moret 1927: 47–52. The evidence is scanty and folkloristic in nature, and the case is far from cogent.

[6] Henri Frankfort, *Cylinder Seals* (London: Macmillan, 1939), p. 100 and plates XVIII h, i, j, XIX b, c, d. Frankfort, moreover, assigns them to the Akkadian period. Deedes cites nothing to support his statement.

[7] See René Labat, *Le caractère religieux de la royauté assyro-babylonienne* (Paris: Adrien-Maisonneuve, 1939), pp. 103–105; Henri Frankfort, *Kingship and the Gods* (University of Chicago Press, 1948), pp. 262–264.

[8] Two chronicle entries tell the story of Enlil-bani, whom King Irra-imitti of Isin placed upon the throne, apparently to serve as *shar-puhi,* since the entries say "that the dynasty might not come to an end." Irra-imitti died during the substitution and Enlil-bani kept the kingship. See L. W. King, *Chronicles Concerning Early Babylonian Kings* (London: Luzac, 1907), II, 12–16, with

immediate surrender of the throne does not in any respect fit Frazer's or Hooke's ritual hypothesis. The substitute was not put to death at the end of his term, but returned entirely whole to his usual routine. Known records show but one *shar-puhi* who was put to death, Damqi, substitute for the late Assyrian king Esarhaddon.[9] On this occasion omens portended the king's death. That is, death threatened the *king*, the man who literally occupied the throne; and by killing a *shar-puhi*, who had been seated on the throne with all the trappings of royalty, the government could circumvent the fates. This occasion reveals the whole purpose of the institution: to deflect threatened dangers from the true king to the substitute king; if harm should strike, it would strike the man on the throne (ordinarily nothing happened to him). The institution can be simply and satisfactorily explained as a magical device for protecting the king. Furthermore the substitution was not periodic and did not occur as part of a New Year ritual (the hypothetical annual sacrifice marked a new year, according to Frazer and his successors).

Frazer did not know about the *shar-puhi* when he wrote *The Golden Bough* (even in the final edition and in *Aftermath*, when he might have had information about this office, he makes no mention of it). He surely would have considered this custom to be his best evidence for an annual sacrifice of divine kings in Mesopotamia, where he was very anxious to find evidence of the institution. It would have provided him with the second stage of his conjectured development of the ritual: real king > substitute king > mock king. He had to be content with a mock king and with such ritual practices as the king's humiliation at the New Year festival. He found his mock king in the Sakaia festival (Frazer 1911b: 113–117), celebrated in Babylon under the Persian domination, and earlier too, if Frazer was right, for he insisted that Sakaia and the ancient Babylonian New Year Festival (the Akitu festival to which he referred as Zakmuk) were one and the same.[10] There are few sources for the Sakaia festival, almost nothing aside from three passages, one each in Strabo, Athenaeus (who cites Berosos and Ktesias), and Dion Chrysostom.[11] In his usual fashion Frazer runs all three together into a single consistent description, which he leads the reader to suppose is vouched for by Berosos, "who as a

discussion in I, 62–68; Labat, *op. cit.*, pp. 103–104, 108–109. This appears to be the tale of Beleûs and Beletaras alluded to by Agathias *Hist.* 2.25, who cites Bion and Alexander Polyhistor. According to H. R. Hall (*The Ancient History of the Near East*, 10th ed. [London: Methuen, 1947], p. 191, note 2), Enlil-bani reigned in Isin about 2184–2160; but the chronicles were composed around 500 B.C. Agathias' Beletaras was identified with Sargon I before the Akkadian chronicles came to light; the mistake may point in the right direction: both Sargon and Enlil-bani were usurpers and a tale was told to legitimate the accession of each. The story of Enlil-bani can hardly be historical as told, since an ordinary *shar-puhi* would surely step down in any case. We may, if we wish, see in it Enlil-bani's plot to take the throne through deception of Irra-imitti.

[9] See Labat, *op. cit*, pp. 103, 359–360.

[10] This meant placing the Sakaia at the vernal equinox, although Berosos (15 Schnabel, *ap*. Ath. 14.639C) placed its first day on the sixteenth of the Macedonian month Lōos, which the available evidence shows to be July or September, a summer month. Frazer (1911b: 116, note 1) seized upon the uncertainty between July and September (he mentions August and October also) to justify his placing the Sakaia in March-April, as his theory required. Andrew Lang (1901: 137–138, 144–146) adequately demonstrated the weakness of Frazer's case. Frazer would have done better to accept the September date and point to evidence that some Mesopotamian cities celebrated the New Year festival at the autumnal equinox; he would then have to interpret Berosos' (or Athenaeus') *Babylon* as Babylonia. Any attempt at etymological identification of Sakaia and Zakmuk is vain.

[11] Berosos *loc. cit.*; Strabo 11.8.5, p. 512; Dion Chrys. 4.66–67; see also Hesych. Σ 65 and Steph. Byz. p. 296 Mein.

Babylonian priest spoke with ample knowledge." Frazer tells us that during the
Sakaia, when masters and servants changed places in Saturnalian revelry, a condemned criminal was dressed in the king's robes, seated on the throne, and given
the title *Zoganês;* for five days he ate and drank luxuriously, enjoyed the king's
concubines, and gave any orders he liked (except, apparently, a commutation of
his death sentence); on the fifth day he was stripped, scourged, and hanged.
Berosos, however, as reported by Athenaeus, mentions only the date and number
of days, the Saturnalian revelry, the title *Zoganês*, and Babylon as the place of
celebration; he says nothing about the criminal or the execution. His Zoganês
is one of the servants in a household (any household, and not the royal palace only),
who ruled the house during the feast and wore royal dress for the period. The
criminal mock king's fatal reign comes from Dion Chrysostom, who puts a description of the feast into the mouth of Diogenes the Cynic in conversation with the
youthful Alexander. Andrew Lang rightly suspected Dion's picture to be fanciful,
since it does not agree with either Berosos' or Strabo's testimony. According to
Strabo, the festival was initiated at Zela in honor of the goddess Anaitis, and was
thereafter celebrated at every shrine of Anaitis; and Zela, rather than Babylon,
appears to be the main seat of the festival. Strabo reports two fundamentally consistent accounts of the origin of the Sakaia: (1) that when Scythians were celebrating at Zela, making use of their spoils to do so, Persian generals set upon them
at night and annihilated them; (2) that when Scythians were revelling upon stores
of food and wine taken in a captured Persian camp, Cyrus and his Persians surprised them and destroyed most of them.[12] Strabo says no more about the festival
than that Persian men and women, dressed in Scythian garb, did a good deal of
drinking and revelling in Bacchic fashion (ἡ τῶν Σακαίων ἑορτὴ Βακχεία τις) ; but
what he does say in no way contradicts the testimony of Berosos-Athenaeus. For
that matter it can be fitted to Dion's account, too; but Strabo says nothing about
Babylon or a condemned criminal who was made mock king and put to death.

Andrew Lang has thoroughly demonstrated both the weakness of the Sakaia
evidence for Frazer's case and Frazer's misuse of this evidence.[13] The festival was
Persian, as its very name indicates: Strabo and Dion call it Persian and say nothing
about Babylon; it is only Athenaeus, citing Berosos' *Babyloniaca,* who mentions
Babylon as the place of celebration; and, of course, Persian kings reigned in Babylon for over two centuries (538–331) .[14] And to find evidence that Iranian kings

---

[12] It is perhaps crass Euhemerism to accept Lang's view (1901:119, 194–195) that the Sakaia
really celebrated a victory in war and was a patriotic festival like the Fourth of July or Guy
Fawkes Day. It should be noticed that Strabo's tale—how Cyrus abandoned a camp full of fine
food and wine to the Scythians and afterwards surprised them in the midst of drunken revels and
destroyed them—repeats Herodotos' tale of how Cyrus tricked the Massagetai (a Scythian people)
beyond the Araxes (1.211). In Strabo the scene is transferred from Turkestan to Pontos, and
Cyrus' success is not followed by his defeat and death. It is an historicized combat myth in which
food and drink are the means whereby either Antagonist or Champion is lured to his doom. In
Polyain. *Strat.* 8.28, Tomyris is a Judith who traps Cyrus in a camp full of food and drink. See
Fontenrose 1959:89, 124, 137, 139–140, 259–260, 488–490.

[13] Lang 1901:76–81, 118–160, 182–199. His criticism of Frazer's case is devastating. He shows too
how impossible it is to find the origin of Purim or of Easter in this Persian festival or to show
any apparentation of Sakaia, Akitu, Purim, and Easter. J. M. Robertson tried valiantly but
unconvincingly to rescue Frazer's case from Lang's attack; see *Pagan Christs,* 2d ed. (London:
Watts, 1911, pp. 144–147); as another ritual theorist he wanted to prove a Judaic mystery drama
which gave rise to the Jesus story.

[14] The title *Zoganês* (which Dion does *not* give to the Sacaean mock king) is perhaps beyond
etymology, but certainly looks like a Greek rendition of a Persian term. Attempts to connect it

were ever put to death annually or periodically is much more difficult than it is to find evidence for the killing of Mesopotamian kings: there is no evidence at all, unless one wishes to consider Dion's account of the Sakaia as evidence.

Next to the Sakaia, Frazer's best evidence is drawn from the program of the Akitu festival. On the fifth day the king went with escort to the Esagil temple: there before Bel's image the high priest took the king's crown, sceptre, and sword from him, slapped his cheek, seized him by the ears, and forced him to bow down before Bel. The king then declared that he had done no wrongful acts during the old year, whereupon the priest returned his royal insignia to him. The priest struck the king's cheek again; if he brought tears to the king's eyes, Bel was favorable; if he did not, dangers impended.[15] This means, say Frazer and Raglan, that formerly the king was actually put to death and his successor installed. But in the absence of confirming evidence, such an interpretation of this ceremony is unnecessary. It can be more easily interpreted as a ceremonial vestige of annual terms for the chief magistrate in the early Mesopotamian city-state—an executive like the Athenian archon or Roman consul—who could be reappointed for another year (unlike the consul) if he could show that he had governed justly and wisely. That suggestion is pure conjecture, although no more so than Frazer's, and it saves the phenomena at least as well. More likely, this ceremony was purely magical in intent, to purify the king of all pollutions accumulated during the preceding year; there is nothing in the ritual text to indicate that it was ever anything but a ceremony of purification and renewal. And it is essential to Frazer's thesis that the king be Bel; but here, we notice, the king exculpates himself before Bel as before another person. He is manifestly not Bel, but Bel's agent.

Much the same conclusion can be drawn about the Egyptian Sed festival, traditionally celebrated after thirty years of a king's reign and then repeated at three-year intervals until his death. At this festival the king's coronation was reenacted. Obviously the ceremony was meant to renew his powers, to give him a new lease of life; nothing in it suggests that it was an innocuous survival of a ritual in which the king was put to death.[16] Moret (1927:51) goes beyond the evidence in interpreting the Sed ritual acts to signify a death and revival of the king.

Raglan, however, still relying principally on Frazer, claims abundant evidence that early Greece had kings who were slain periodically. He says, "But whereas the existing accounts of the ritual of Egypt and Mesopotamia provide only for a pretence of killing the king, the traditions of Greece and less civilized countries point to a ritual in which the king was actually killed, . . . annually, [or] at the end of some longer term, . . . " (*H* xiv). For Greece, he tells us, it was usually an eight-year term. His evidence is that section of *The Golden Bough* in which Frazer cites eight-year cycles in Greek rituals, customs, and myths (Frazer 1911b: 58–60, 68–83, 87–92). At best this is evidence for royal terms of eight years, but all of it is legendary or inferred from ritual practices—yet Raglan has strictly forbidden us to rely on legend as historical evidence, and the inferences alone

---

with Semitic words, as with Hebrew *sagan* (which means "captain" or "nobleman") are very dubious; e.g., Robertson, *op. cit.*, pp. 159–160.

[15] Text (trans. A. Sachs) in *Ancient Near Eastern Texts,* ed. J. B. Pritchard (Princeton University Press, 1950), pp. 331–334. See Fontenrose 1959:436–446.

[16] On the Sed festival see Frankfort, *Kingship and the Gods,* pp. 79–88; see also J. Černy, *Ancient Egyptian Religion* (London: Hutchinson, 1952), pp. 122–123.

lead to circular reasoning. There is no historical record of a Greek king who suffered a ritual death at the end of an eight-year term or any other kind of term; and there is absolutely no historical or archaeological evidence that in prehistoric Greece "the king must die." In fact, there is no mythical record either of just that. Frazer cites eight-year cycles in myth and tradition without any king-killing and mythical murders of kings that were not periodic or sacrificial; he gives the appearance of having a good deal of evidence for eight-year reigns by introducing long digressions on shooting stars, animal transformations, and the like.

There is, moreover, no record of divine kingship in ancient Greece. As H. J. Rose (1959:371–378) admirably demonstrated in his examination of the case which A. B. Cook had made in his *Zeus* for Frazerian divine kings in early Greece, there is nothing besides the equivocal evidence of myths and legends (and little in them); that Greek kings exercised priestly functions proves nothing, especially since priests were not gods.[17] Rose ignores the occasional Homeric phrase in which it is said of a king that his people honored him as a god. Lest anyone see divine kings in this expression, it should be said that if the king were a god, the *as (hōs)* would not be used. This adverb plainly indicates a simile: it is not used appositively like the English *as.* The Homeric kings like Agamemnon and Odysseus are plainly mortal men on a lower level than the gods and are at the mercy of deity.

ETHNOGRAPHIC EVIDENCE FOR KING SACRIFICE

In all the ancient world we find no record, clear or obscure, of an annual or periodic sacrifice of divine kings. That leaves us with the ethnographic evidence, the rituals and customs of contemporary and recent "savages," as Frazer and Raglan constantly call them. Raglan triumphantly tells us that Frazer cites hundreds of instances. True enough, Frazer (1911b:14–58) offers a goodly number of examples of king-killing, mostly from Africa. He could, and would, have added many more examples if he had written *The Dying God* in recent years, for in Tor Irstam's *The King of Ganda* (1944) most of the relevant African material on king-killing is conveniently assembled—the practice is alleged for fifty African peoples. In none, however, is the king killed annually, and the examples of periodic king-killing are rare and dubious. Still, the ritualists say, here are kings put to death when their strength fails, a custom which preserves the original meaning of the ritual; the old rigidity and excessive caution of periodic sacrifice have given way to a more rational irregularity. And since the king-killing custom is so prevalent in Africa, they say, it must either have spread southward from Egypt or have had the same origin as the hypothetical Egyptian custom (Hamitic, according to Seligman 1934). And indeed the most remarkable instance attested occurs (or occurred) among the Shilluk of the Nilotic Sudan. Frazer depended upon the first studies of the Shilluk made by C. G. Seligman, who lived among them and re-

---

[17] A. B. Cook, *Zeus: A Study in Ancient Religion* (Cambridge University Press, 1914–40), I, 12–14, 79–81; II, 794, 1073–1077, 1087–1089, 1121–1137, 1159–1160; III, 733–734. See Marlow 1961, who finds no good evidence of the Hooke-Raglan myth-ritual pattern nor of divine kings in early Greece, and who demolishes the theory of Raglan and others that the Homeric epics were ritual texts which accompanied a ritual performance called "Trojan War." I should also mention Arne Furumark, "Was There a Sacral Kingship in Minoan Crete?" (*Studies in the History of Religions,* IV [1959], 369–370); his answer to the question of his title is affirmative, but on inadequate and ambiguous evidence; and he interprets the Palaikastro hymn as a ritual text (see chapter ii below).

ported that they still practiced king-killing, although no instance occurred during his stay. According to Seligman, the god Nyakang is immanent in every Shilluk king; the Shilluk believe that if the king should become sick or feeble, his weakness would infect the people, cattle, and crops; and "there is no doubt that the kings of the Shilluk were killed ceremonially when they began to show signs of old age or ill-health, . . . "[18] Seligman was told that in contemporary practice certain chiefs and nobles, having decided that the king (*reth*) must die, informed him of his fate and took him to a hut (especially built for the occasion) and strangled him (Seligman rejects another account received from informants, that the king's wives did the strangling). After two months the king-killing cabal broke the hut down, buried the king's bones, and then for the first time informed the Shilluk people of the king's death. The people wept, slaughtered cattle, and sacrificed a man and woman by drowning them. The Shilluk reported that five generations earlier they had abandoned a custom of walling the king and a "nubile maiden" in a hut without food or water.[19]

For the moment let us grant that the Shilluk kill (and have killed) their kings in the aforesaid ways. But where is that elaborate ritual which Raglan describes in great detail? Where are the symbolic destruction of the old world in flood or fire, the ritual combat, the construction of a new world and a new mankind from the dead king's body and blood, and the sacred marriage? There is no ritual to speak of: an aging or sick ruler is taken to a hut (apparently at night) and strangled. Everything is done in secret; there is no public fanfare such as Frazer's or Raglan's theory demands. The later slaughter of cattle and of two persons, who were bound in a canoe that was loaded with various objects and then sunk in the river, hardly meets the hypothetical ritual; moreover Seligman owed his information about this sacrifice not to his own informants, but to a Shilluk folklore text in Westermann's collection. However the king dies, the king's successor is installed with great pomp after an interregnum of one year. Coronations are always splendid affairs, and this coronation can hardly be taken to be the enactment of resurrection or re-creation, as demanded by Raglan's ritual scheme. His whole ritual should take place in one festival, whereas among the Shilluk the old king's death, the human sacrifices (if the report be accepted), and the new king's installation take place at widely separate times, occupying a whole year from first to last. Seligman points to the report of a still more ancient custom in which we may see combat for the kingship between the king and a challenger. A royal son had the right to attempt the king's life, and if he killed the king, to reign in his stead. Royal sons made the attempt only at night when the king was alone and almost unguarded in his harem; but ever on the watch, like Frazer's King of the Woods, he prowled about all night, fully armed, ready for any challenger who should appear. If the report is anything more than traditional lore,

---

[18] See Seligman 1932: 90–93. This book is later than *The Dying God,* but it repeats the results of Seligman's studies that Frazer used. Notice the past tense in the quoted sentence and also the words, "the Shilluk kings are (or were) killed," which indicate uncertainty about its being a contemporary sacrifice.

[19] For this sacrifice Seligman cites Diedrich Westermann, *The Shilluk People* (Philadelphia: Board of Foreign Missions, United Presbyterian Church; Berlin: Reimer [Ernst Vohsen], 1912), p. 136, a text dictated by a Shilluk informant. In this text two girls are walled in a hut with the *dead* body of the king (the cause of his death is not given) and die there.

it may be a memory of regicides and usurpations, which have nothing to do with king sacrifice; in any case we observe none of the ritual of periodic renewal that Hooke and Raglan have constructed.

Frazer (and his sources), Seligman, Irstam, and others cite identical or similar practices among other African peoples: Dinka, Konde, Bakitara, Bungoro, Kibanga, Zulu, and over forty others.[20] In all parts of the continent, it appears, kings, on showing signs of weakness, have been strangled or compelled to drink poison; as among the Shilluk, an interregnum of several months followed the king's death (not reported to the people for a time), ending with the installation of a successor. Thus there appears to be abundant evidence for the killing of kings in Africa, although it is hardly evidence for the Frazer-Hooke-Raglan rituals. Yet the reader should notice one constant statement made in the material on the killing of the divine king in Africa as reported by the aforesaid scholars. In every instance, save that of the Shilluk, the native informants said that the king *used to be* killed, and that the practice came to an end at some indefinite time in the past, two, three, or more generations back. If, then, the information is reliable, we should expect that African divine kings were meeting ritual deaths two or three centuries ago and that early visitors to Africa might have witnessed or heard about king-killing as a contemporary practice. But even the earliest European visitors were told that the killing of kings was a practice of earlier times. Dos Santos, a Portuguese traveller who visited Bantu tribes of Mozambique in the sixteenth century, reported concerning the king of Sofala that "It was formerly the custom of the kings of this land to commit suicide by taking poison when any disaster or natural physical defect fell upon them, such as impotence, infectious disease, . . . " (Seligman 1934:30). In truth, we can go back another sixteen centuries to Diodoros of Sicily (3.5–7), whose testimony about the kings of Aethiopia has been used by Frazer and the ritualists as an important link between ancient Egyptian and modern African king-killing, especially since Diodoros' reference to kings and priests at Meroe brings us near to the Shilluk and Dinka. Diodoros, relying upon a source that might be some two centuries earlier, informs us that whenever the priests at Meroe took the notion, they sent a message to the king, instructing him to kill himself, since the gods had so ordered. Every king obeyed the divine behest until the time of Ptolemy II in Egypt, when King Ergamenes of Aethiopia refused to obey the command and killed the priests instead. Once more the custom *used to be* practiced; and the report contains a legend of how the practice came to an end. Diodoros (3.7) then goes on to report the court etiquette of Aethiopians. When a king lost the use of some part of his body, his companions gave up that member in sympathy. This custom, whether or not it is reliably reported, is directly contrary to the reported custom of killing kings when they failed in health or wholeness. Obviously an eyeless, toothless, or legless king would have a bad effect on his land and should be sacrificed as soon as possible; yet among a people who reputedly killed their kings, and in a section of Africa where king-killing has reputedly been traditional, Diodoros' lame kings lived out their lives and without objection imposed their own disabilities on their subjects.

---

[20] Frazer 1911*b*: 14–41, Seligman 1934: 21–39, Irstam 1944: 142–146; Leo Frobenius, *Und Afrika Sprach* . . . III (Berlin: Vita, Deutsches Verlagshaus, 1913), pp. 84–87, 113, 140–143, 147, 255; E. J. and J. D. Krige, *The Realm of a Rain-Queen* (Oxford University Press, 1943), pp. 165–166.

So constantly is it said that the killing of kings "used to be," and so unverifiable is the rare report of contemporary king-killing, that one may conclude that the whole reported tradition of African king-killing is itself mythical, a fragment or memory of an ancient African myth. Such was the conclusion which I had already reached when I came upon Evans-Pritchard's *The Divine Kingship of the Shilluk of the Nilotic Sudan* (1948) and found it confirmed. In spite of Seligman's unhesitating acceptance of the Shilluk tradition that failing kings were put to death, Evans-Pritchard says, "I must confess that I consider [the Shilluk statements] of interest more as an indication of the mystical nature of the kingship than as evidence that the kings were, in fact, ever killed in the ways mentioned or for the reasons given" (p. 20). He found no convincing evidence that the Shilluk ever observed such a custom; therefore, he adds, "In the absence of other than traditional evidence of royal executions in Shilluk history and in view of the contradictory accounts cited I conclude that the ceremonial putting to death of kings is probably a fiction, ... "(p. 21). Shilluk kings have, of course, been killed in the usual secular ways, by assassins or by rebels in battle. So if the case for Shilluk king-killing fails, it fails *a fortiori* for other African peoples. We look in vain for an authentic royal victim, whether real king or substitute king, whether strangled or poisoned or killed in combat by a sanctioned challenger. And even if the reports are true, we still do not see either Raglan's ritual pattern or any clear relation to rituals of the ancient Near East; nor, so far as I know, do we find any African myth which the reported king-killing has manifestly inspired. Indeed the African myths of kingship are quite otherwise.

Today we know more about African kingship than Frazer knew a half-century ago, when anthropologists gave little attention to primitive government. Recently several books on African tribal government have appeared, written by distinguished anthropologists.[21] These books necessarily say a good deal about the powers, terms, prerogatives, and duties of native kings and chieftains in those African societies which trained observers have studied; but one will hunt almost in vain for any mention of the institution which Frazer, Raglan, and others have emphasized so much. In *African Political Systems* (p. 137) we learn that the Mugabe of Ankole drank poison when his physical powers waned (an instance unknown to Frazer). This too is reported as a *former* custom. The Nyakyusa (southern Tanganyika) killing of a ritual king and the killing of a mock king at Nyoro accession ceremonies are likewise reported as *past* customs.[22] Frazer, moreover, who uncritically accepted the reports of unskilled observers, was wrong in some instances, e.g., concerning the Zulu. He believed (1911*b*: 36–37) that King Chaka was destined to a ritual death when his powers waned; but in fact the Zulu killed Chaka, not "ritually," but because he had oppressed his people. This is evidence of secular rebellion and regicide, not of the ritual death of a divine king, and similar instances can be adduced. According to Max Gluckman, even secular regicide is rare among Africans: "It required a long period of suffering before the

---

[21] Notably Fortes and Evans-Pritchard 1940; Mair 1962; I. Schapera, *Government and Politics in Tribal Societies* (London: Watts, 1956). Schapera's book is limited to South African peoples, Mair's to East African.

[22] See Mair 1962: 224–227. Reports of human sacrifices at Nyoro and Ganda accession ceremonies and at intervals in a reign to augment the king's strength (Mair 1962: 224–225) also refer to an obsolete custom.

people would turn against their rulers" (Fortes and Evans-Pritchard 1940:42). Bantu and Nilote, we see, differ in no way from Frenchman and Russian in this respect (did Louis XVI and Nicholas II suffer ritual deaths?).

If one turns from recent anthropological studies of African tribal government to like studies of African tribal religion, one finds no firmer support for Frazer's case. In *African Traditional Religion* (1954), Geoffrey Parrinder mentions only the "destooling" of chiefs among the Ashanti and Dahomeans, and the Yoruba practice of "[giving a] chief parrot's eggs as a sign that he must commit suicide" (p. 74). These are not ritual deaths, as Parrinder reports them, but political devices for removing kings. Thus West African institutions offer Frazer no more comfort than do East and South African.

Miss Mair, in fact, spends a few pages (229–233) on Frazer's theory and asserts that no "East African ruler . . . conforms at all points to Frazer's picture of the divine king," and we may extend her statement to all Africa. Africa has divine kings and ritual kings; African kings have ritual duties; Africans believe that the king's health is sympathetically linked to his nation's welfare. But there is no evidence for the ritual killing of the divine king.

Miss Mair (226–227, 232) is inclined to accept the Nyakyusa tradition of a former killing of a ritual king in anticipation of his natural death on the ground that the old men give such circumstantial accounts of the act: "When a Nyakyusa king was dying his councillors stopped up the orifices of his body so that his soul should not escape and the fertility of the land with it." As Mair points out, "this happened *when he was dying*—not when he was simply thought to be not as strong as he was." What happened to the Nyakyusa ritual king (no one now holds the office), as Mair reports it, conforms very closely to a widespread African custom of not allowing a dying king to breathe out his last breath by himself. Edwin Loeb reports this custom among the Kuanyama: before the king can die "naturally" a faithful attendant smothers him and does so at the last moment possible. This is essentially what Mair reports as a former Nyakyusa practice: the Nyakyusa councillors prevented the king's soul, identified with the fertility of the land, from escaping. According to Loeb, the Kuanyama identify the king's last breath with his soul; and if they do not catch his soul, his successor will be weakened: "If the heir caused a dying king to be killed, he then possessed the king's soul and became, like his predecessors, the incarnation of Kalunga, the High God. If on the other hand a king was allowed to die an entirely natural death, his soul did not enter into his successor."[23] This practice of anticipating the king's last breath hardly supports Frazer's theory. This is not the killing of a king when he begins to show signs of weakness, but when he is all but dead; it is not periodic, and there is no ritual. The attendants observe rules of etiquette, and the king must be suffocated in a prescribed way: e.g., the Kuanyama smother him with a piece of lambskin. All this is very far from Frazer's or Hooke's or Raglan's sacrificial ritual. Even this killing of the dying king is generally reported as a former custom, although Loeb and others believe that it still prevails among some tribes. Granting this to be a genuine African custom, we can see in it a source of those traditions

[23] Edwin M. Loeb, *In Feudal Africa* (Bloomington: Indiana University, Research Center in Anthropology, Folklore, and Linguistics, 1962), p. 28.

reported or collected by Seligman, Frazer, Irstam, and others.[24] Another source may be assassinations and usurpations, when the man who challenges the reigning king and succeeds in killing him obviously has the power to win the nation's acceptance of himself as successor. That is, these traditions are the myths and beliefs that justify and validate (see pp. 57–59, below) the actual killing of kings by whatever method and for whatever reason. Out of this traditional lore came those fanciful reports that fill a large part of *The Dying God*.

If we look outside Africa for evidence of king-killing, Frazer's hypothesis fares no better. There is in fact little to be found. Frazer, relying on the reports of early travellers to southern India, cites kings of Quilacare and Calicut as rulers who had to kill themselves at the end of a twelve-year reign.[25] A Portuguese traveller in the early sixteenth century reported that a king in Quilacare, after reigning twelve years, feasted the Brahmans and then in their presence mounted a scaffold and started hacking away his own members and flesh, finally cutting his throat as he grew faint from loss of blood; then scaffold and corpse were burned. The traveller did not see this done; he reported only what he was told.[26] According to Hamilton, an English traveller who visited Malabar in 1695, this royal suicide had *once* been the custom in Calicut. As a contemporary custom, he reported a feast of ten or twelve days held every twelve years. At the end of the festival any four men who wished could try to kill the king in his tent and take the kingship. The catch was that thirty or forty thousand armed men guarded the king's tent; yet there were always a few men who were ready to commit suicide by attacking the king's guard on that day. Hamilton did not witness this event, although he was in the region at the time. This custom was last observed in 1743, according to Logan, who found a record of it in the royal archives of Calicut. Logan, however, makes no mention of an earlier royal suicide. The king's suicide is plainly another "used to be" custom and almost certainly a fiction. We cannot be certain, either, that the reported later custom is authentic; a description of it in royal archives is no guarantee of its actuality: Logan examined the archives more than a century after the alleged final observance. Nevertheless, let all reports be as true as you please; where is the Hooke-Hocart-Raglan ritual? We see only feasting followed by the king's suicide on a scaffold, followed in turn by cremation of the dead king's body and election of a new king. In the later custom we see only a futile attack on the king's bodyguard.

Wherever we look we reach the same result. Frazer (1911*b*: 51–52) cites the

---

[24] I have grave doubts that the alleged anticipatory killing of a dying king is or has been a real custom; no one has actually confirmed it. I am inclined to believe that the reports of this custom too are part of African folklore, fragments of the king-killing myth conjectured above. In Ghana, for example, the Akan king's death meant that the cosmos had succumbed to chaos; however old or sick the king was, his death was not anticipated. The cemetery custodian was sometimes brought to a dying king's bed, for the Akan believed that this would cause the king to die sooner; the custodian, however, merely touched the king gently and spoke a word of sympathy. See Meyerowitz 1960:186–196.

[25] Frazer (1911*b*:46–51) relies on F. de Magalhães, *A Description of the Coasts of East Africa and Malabar* (title of the English translation published by Hakluyt Society, London, 1866, vol. 35, pp. 172–173; the original has been wrongly attributed to Duarte Barbosa) and on A. Hamilton, *Account of the East Indies* in Pinkerton's *Voyages and Travels*, VIII, 374; also on William Logan, *Malabar* (Madras, 1887).

[26] We may notice that the Portuguese traveller speaks of kings in Quilacare, whereas Hamilton and Logan speak of kings in Calicut. In Quilacare it was the king of the province, who was subject to the king of Colam. Apparently the greater king suffered no ritual death.

king of Passier in Sumatra: he too was killed after a short reign *in former times*. Frazer's example of the kingship of Bengal (1911*b*: 51) points to frequent assassi-nations rather than to ritual deaths (reports on the kingship of Passier also look rather like assassinations and usurpations): not all kings were killed. In any land an assassin-usurper who succeeds in gaining power is likely to be accepted and acknowledged by palace attendants and subjects. Other examples of human vic-tims (e.g., the Meriah of Khonds) that Frazer cites were not kings, chiefs, pontiffs, or rainmakers; nor is their any indication that the victims were royal surrogates. Outside of Africa and South Asia, Frazer found no evidence of king-killing which is not purely mythical or legendary. Moreover he cites many instances of tem-porary kings and mock kings who were not put to death.

Such is Frazer's evidence on which Raglan relies for his original ritual, and which has deeply impressed Raglan, Graves, Hyman, and many another. For Frazer's impressive accumulation of materials has overwhelmed them, as it has many readers (especially the earlier), and blinded them to his frequent non-sequiturs and to the weaknesses in his argument. But in the past quarter-century an increasing number of readers, especially anthropologists, folklorists, and classi-cal scholars, have not been convinced.[27]

PRIMEVAL ORIGINS

Thus *The Golden Bough* fails to provide Raglan with the evidence he needs for his Ur-ritual of king-killing. Raglan's own theory, in so far as he goes beyond Frazer in tracing all myth and religion back to a single origin in the ancient Near East, encounters obstacles which Frazer's did not. We must ask about the ages before Raglan's primeval ritual began. Was it derived from earlier rituals? Raglan grants that there were earlier rituals, e.g., among late palaeolithic men, "but the rituals of known religions are not derived from [them]" (*OR* 51). Yet our only reason for interpreting the sorcerer painting at Les Trois Frères Cave (a man masked as a deer or elk) as a participant in a ritual is that persons so masked take part in known primitive rituals (which, according to Raglan, must be descended from the ancient Near Eastern ritual). But let Raglan have his way. His theory requires that there be no myth or ritual on hand in the ancient Near East when the first divine victim was sacrificed. This sacrifice occurred, he says, in an already centralized kingdom (*H* xiii *fin.*). So it could not have begun before 4000 B.C. (*OR* 68). If we allow his king-sacrifice to begin in a monarchical city-state we might push the date back toward 6000 B.C. (much too early). We must assume that in the preceding centuries and millennia men told no stories, since in Raglan's hypothesis all known traditional tales must be derived from his Ur-

---

[27] For critiques of Frazer see Lang 1901, Fontenrose 1962: 76–77, and E. R. Leach, "Golden Bough or Gilded Twig?," *Daedalus* (Spring 1961), pp. 371–387. The anonymous reviewer of Evans-Pritchard's *Essays in Social Anthropology* in the London *Times Literary Supplement* (September 20, 1963, p. 698) points out the fundamental reason for the persistent vogue of Frazer's views among non-specialists: Evans-Pritchard's "account of the Shilluk kingship . . . is more complex and, from a European point of view, more prosaic than Frazer's mystique of the dying priest-king yielding to a young successor who will restore the national vitality. It is not difficult to understand why many general readers will continue to prefer the Frazerian type of interpretation which pro-vides them with instant poetry, to the better argued, better documented and intellectually more exacting constructs of modern students." Greenway (1964:283) makes the same point. Error is indeed hard to combat and almost impossible to defeat finally, especially if the undisciplined con-sider it "poetic"; yet it always turns out to be as tinsel compared with gold.

ritual and only from that; and if traditional tales were already current, how deny that they must have had some influence on the content of the myths which arose from the ritual? Could it be that men had speech and yet told no stories? When did human speech begin? Surely the cave painters had speech; and there is much in palaeolithic artifacts to indicate that their makers and users gave instructions in words.[28] We may safely assume that Magdalenian hunters were speaking in 12,000 B.C. So if we allow the most favorable dates to Raglan's hypothesis at each end, we are left with 6,000 years in which men could talk but never told a story to one another.[29]

Raglan would grant, I suppose, that men reported exciting events to friends, who repeated them to others, and that these narratives became changed and distorted in transmission. Raglan tells us that this sort of thing can happen: "a garbled account becomes more garbled every time it is repeated"; "the stories of court life that get abroad today are always inaccurate and often quite untrue" (*H* i). He would probably grant that supernatural features can enter into such narratives. Then are not these narratives what we call legends (which Raglan derives only from myths)? No, Raglan replies; some people call them legends, but they are really pseudo-history; they die out of oral tradition in a century or so and never contribute anything to myth or ritual. It appears that myth and pseudo-history are mutually repulsive, never touching each other. Myth and legend, according to Raglan, never contain any historical truth or real persons: if the Mesopotamians or Egyptians of 6000-4000 B.C. told pseudo-historical tales, these had no effect on the momentous ritual text, i.e., myth, which they invented, even if some tales were told about the king.

Still, Raglan must hedge. Attila, Theodoric, and Charlemagne were certainly historical persons, and yet they appear prominently as characters in medieval legends. Raglan says that they have slipped into the place of old hero-gods (*H* v). Recalling, however, what Raglan has said about Arthur, Robin Hood, Agamemnon, and other legendary figures, we know well that if the historicity of Attila, Theodoric, and Charlemagne were not guaranteed, Raglan (and Hyman too) would confidently assert that they were simply old gods and that anybody who thought otherwise would be a Euhemerist. That is, the only real persons who have ever become legendary figures are those whose historicity can be proved. I do not believe in the historicity of Arthur or Agamemnon either (I am not arguing for an origin of legends in real events and persons), but I believe that Raglan's way of proving them unhistorical is unsound.

THOMAS BECKET

The weakness of Raglan's theory is revealed when he deals with Thomas Becket and Guy Fawkes (1955). The murder of Becket in Canterbury Cathedral on

---

[28] See Jacquetta Hawkes, *History of Mankind I: Prehistory* (New York: Harper & Row, 1963), pp. 108–113; Grahame Clark, *World Prehistory: An Outline* (Cambridge University Press, 1961), pp. 28–29, 33.

[29] Raglan has a ritual theory of language origin too (*OR* 44, 45–46). Ritualists are likely to seize on the gesture theory of speech origin to support their position; in doing so they identify all gesture with ritual, just as they sometimes incline to identify all speech with myth. But obviously, if all gesture is ritual and all speech is myth, the terms *ritual* and *myth* lose all distinctive meaning, and the ritual theory, embracing everything, becomes meaningless. Then we must start all over to study ceremonial acts as distinct from other acts, traditional tales of gods and heroes as distinct from all other forms of speech.

December 29, 1170, is an historical event, described by five eyewitnesses who wrote accounts of the deed (Abbott 1898: I, 11–15). A cult of the Martyr Thomas (canonized as St. Thomas of Canterbury on February 21, 1173) began at once in Canterbury and flourished there until the Reformation. After 1220 the cathedral contained four shrines of St. Thomas (Martyrdom, his tomb in the crypt, St. Thomas's crown, the great shrine).[30] Hither came thousands of pilgrims for three centuries and a half. A Canterbury pilgrimage provided Chaucer with the frame of his *Canterbury Tales*, and the poet lets us see vividly how

> ... to Caunterbury they wende,
> The holy blisful martir for to seke,
> That hem hath holpen, whan that they were seke.
>
> (Prologue 16–18)

Thomas immediately acquired a healing cult; his first miracles, reported soon after his death (the very first is reported to have occurred the evening that followed his murder), are miracles of healing. Like Asklepios, he appeared to the sick in dreams and prescribed remedies to them. Thousands were healed, according to report, by drinking St. Thomas's water, which had remarkable powers; it was drawn from St. Thomas's well in the crypt and tinctured with what was reputed to be his blood. And, like Asklepios, Thomas even raised men from death (so we are told by William of Canterbury and others).[31] He was also a savior and protector of sailors and seafarers, and thus his cult resembles those of Apollo and the Hemithea of Kastabos, who were also believed powerful for both healing and safe navigation.[32] Like Poseidon, Thomas could strike the earth with his staff

---

[30] J. Charles Wall, *The Four Shrines of St. Thomas at Canterbury* (London: Talbot, 1932); John Morris, *The Life and Martyrdom of Saint Thomas Becket*, 2d ed. (London, New York, 1885), pp. 473–476.

[31] See Abbott 1898: I, 250–251; II, 18, 44, 51, 55. For the testimonies of the Asklepios cult at Epidauros, see Emma J. and Ludwig Edelstein, *Asclepius I: Testimonies* (Baltimore: Johns Hopkins Press, 1945).

[32] *Hemithea* (Demigoddess) was a name or title of the Aegean sea-goddess commonly called Leukothea (White Goddess); see my *White Goddess and Syrian Goddess*, University of California Publications in Semitic Philology, XI (Berkeley and Los Angeles: University of California Press, 1951), 125–148, and Diod. 5.62, where we see Apollo as the divine patron of the three daughters of Staphylos who were translated into forms of the sea-goddess. In fact, the latter myth (or its type) appears to survive in several Canterbury miracle stories wherein a young woman replaces Hemithea. See e.g., Abbott 1898: II, 237–256: Salerna of Ifield stole cheese from her mother's larder, and in fear of punishment leaped into a well. The daughters of Staphylos fell asleep while guarding their father's wine (perhaps because they drank of it), and as they slept swine broke into the wine vat and destroyed its contents; in fear of punishment they leaped into the sea. St. Thomas appeared to Salerna and protected her until rescue came; Apollo appeared to Staphylos' daughters in the sea and brought them safely to land. In the miracle tales of men who were buried under earth or submerged under water we may see Hemithea-Leukothea's male companion, son or brother, worshipped as Palaimon or Tenes or Anios, and closely related to Dionysos, Attis, and Adonis—the descent into earth or sea in the pagan myths means death, which is followed by resurrection and apotheosis. William of Gloucester, buried under a fall of earth from the tenth hour of one day to the third hour of the next (two days in archaic reckoning) emerged alive and unhurt with St. Thomas's help, after the priest had celebrated his funeral rites (Abbott, II, 220–235); just so Herakles, who had the by-name Palaimon, emerged from the Nemean lion's cave to find King Molorchos making funeral offerings to the dead Herakles (see Fontenrose 1959: 357). John of Roxburgh, cast by his horse into the Tweed, descended into the depths of the stream to a rock-built hollow: *in quoddam concavum lapideum quod vel natura construxerat vel suo naufrago martyr excavaverat intrusus est* (William of Canterbury). He stayed underneath for many hours, saw visions, and finally was raised miraculously to land; he too had been given up for dead (Abbott, II, 259–270). Only in this sketchy way can I draw the parallels here; the correspondences of detail between these miracle stories and the indicated pagan myths are numerous and deserve careful study.

and bring forth a spring. Like healing and marine deities of the pagans, he had prophetic powers: he had reputedly foreseen his violent death and he spoke prophecies in dreams after his death. The cult of St. Thomas of Canterbury (or of Acre) spread throughout England, and in France, Italy, Flanders, and elsewhere churches were dedicated to him. Relics of St. Thomas could be seen everywhere, and some can still be seen; the four shrines at Canterbury held his bones, his arms could once be seen in a nunnery in Lisbon, and churches at Mons and Florence still have parts of his arms.[33]

Although the cult of St. Thomas waned after Henry VIII destroyed the shrines and relics at Canterbury in 1538, it has by no means disappeared. The Roman Catholic Church maintains the cult: at Canterbury the Catholic church of St. Thomas contains a reproduction of the great shrine. Nor has the Church of England entirely forsaken him. Thirty-seven Anglican churches have preserved their dedications to St. Thomas of Canterbury (e.g., at Lapford in Devon), and the verger at Canterbury Cathedral now guides visitors to the sites of the former shrines. In several English towns and districts St. Thomas's Day, July 7, is still observed with fairs, feasts, and customs, either on the day itself or on the Sunday or Monday following.[34]

Myths and legends soon gathered about Thomas. Not only are the tales of miracles and cures abundant, but also marvelous features found their way into the saint's biography, even in the contemporary *vitae*. Marvels attended his birth, every phase of his life, and his death; obviously some biographers adapted Thomas's *vita* to the gospel narrative. The tale of the murder reached Iceland in the thirteenth century and became the subject of the *Thomas Saga*, a highly inconvenient fact for Lord Raglan, who contends that all Norse sagas have plots derived from the *Volsunga Saga* (*H* v).

So we see clearly that in the tradition of Thomas Becket an historical person became an object of worship and a figure of myth and legend. Obviously, if the historicity of Thomas Becket were not unassailable, Raglan would banish him from history as merely a medieval form of Asklepios or Apollo. In making this point I do not intend to say that gods and heroes were originally living men, or that we should look for the source of myths and legends in true history. I am *not* advocating "Euhemerism"; I am showing that historical persons sometimes become objects of cult and figures of legend, and that historical events may become episodes of legend. If we dismiss the miracle legends as pure fabrications, we still find legendary distortion of the murder narrative. For example, according

---

[33] Latin texts and translations of the accounts of miracles compiled by Benedict and William of Canterbury are contained in Abbott 1898: II; for illustrative examples see 76–79, 80–102, 128–143, 146–160, 162–169. On the miracles in general see Abbott, I, 223–333, and II, 3–75; Morris, *op. cit.*, pp. 454–465; Francis Watt, *Canterbury Pilgrims and Their Ways* (London: Methuen, 1917), pp. 24–34; H. Snowden Ward, *The Canterbury Pilgrimages* (London: Black, 1927), pp. 85–92. On relics, pilgrimages, and cult see Morris, pp. 466–477, 510–519; Watt, pp. 35–46, 160–174; Ward, pp. 100–107.

[34] On the modern cult see Watt, *op. cit.*, pp. 274–276; Ward, *op. cit.*, *pp.* 103–107; A. R. Wright and T. E. Lones, *British Calendar Customs, England III: Fixed Festivals* (London: Glaisher; Glasgow: Wylie, 1940), pp. 30–32. Wright describes the Bodmin Riding, celebrated at Bodmin in Cornwall on the Sunday and Monday after July 7 with a riding procession, offering of flowers at the Priory, and drinking of "the Riding-ale," which two young men, attended by musicians, carried around the town. The observance apparently died out in the nineteenth century, unless it has been revived, as such customs often are nowadays.

to William Fitzstephen, when the four knights tried to drag Thomas from the cathedral, he struggled against them and his companions held him back; and so the knights killed him on the spot (Abbott 1898: I 102–104, 128). According to Edward Grim, Thomas clung to a pillar, so that the murderers could not move him (Abbot 1898: I, 101–102). According to an anonymous account, Edward Grim held Thomas back, thwarting the efforts of the assassins to drag him outside (Abbott 1898: I, 107). But in the *Thomas Saga* the knights could not budge Thomas, because the Holy Ghost made the marble floor as soft as snow, so that Thomas's feet were firmly planted in the marble; and as evidence of this marvel, adds the *Saga,* his footprints may still be seen on the floor and receive the pilgrims' kisses (Abbott 1898: I, 114–115). The knight's first blow, dealt by Reginald Fitzurse, fell on Edward Grim's arm, which was nearly amputated (Abbott 1898: I, 128). No recovery of the arm is mentioned in contemporary sources; but according to pseudo-Grim, it was miraculously made whole a year later, after Grim had despaired of its healing, when the martyr appeared to him in a dream (Abbott 1898: II, 288). In the *Saga* Grim's arm was miraculously "whole and healed before the body of the Archbishop was cold on the floor" (Abbott 1898: I, 245).

In these accounts we notice the very process which Raglan and Hyman deny, the legendary distortion of an actual event and the introduction or addition of supernatural features to an historical narrative. In truth, we may plainly see two sources of legend in the Becket material. (1) The miracles and visions, which have no basis in actual events, were modelled on familiar patterns of Christian myth and legend: the Christ story and saints' legends directly affected the Thomas story. Old pagan myths, long since absorbed into Christian legend, affected it indirectly—myths of Asklepios, Leukothea-Hemithea, and Dionysos (see notes 31, 32). This is not to deny that these myth-types may have an ultimate ritual origin—that is the main question before us. (2) Most legends about Becket's life and death obviously arose from actual events, and some miracle legends possibly have a basis in fact (the Canterbury clergy made some attempt to verify the early cures, and the same question of authenticity arises as for tales of faith healings in general). We may grant that the historical narratives were gradually shaped into traditional forms of legend; but we must still allow that an actual event, or series of events, made Thomas Becket a figure of legend and shaped the central narrative of his death in those accounts that are legendary rather than historical.

We can hardly overvalue the Becket material for the study of myth and religion: it allows us to witness the birth and development of a deity, his cult, and his myth. Are we to say that Thomas's case is unique? That nothing of the sort happened in ancient times? We may observe, above all, that although the cult and myth grew up together, there is no correspondence whatever between the rituals of Thomas worship and the mythical events. We may overlook Lord Raglan's inconsistency and allow him to say that in this instance the myth recounts an historical event: "As the pilgrims performed the ritual of touring the cathedral and singing hymns or praying at spots connected with Becket's life and death, the story of these was recited. The story, since it explained the ritual, could properly be described as a myth" (1955:76). But do the tour, hymns, and prayers re-enact the tale of murder in the cathedral? Or did the myth grow up with or develop out of the rituals as their spoken accompaniment, as Raglan says all myths do? Obviously in this case the myth is prior; and the processions, hymns, prayers, offerings, and masses at Canterbury were the long-established forms of Catholic worship. What Raglan needs at Canterbury is a dramatic ritual or ritual drama which enacted Becket's ministry, passion, death, and epiphany as a saint, out of which drama the myth as we know it took shape. No such thing occurred.

GUY FAWKES

If in the tradition of Thomas Becket we witness the making of a god (i.e., a benevolent deity), in the tradition of Guy Fawkes we witness the making of a demon (a malevolent deity).[35] Guy Fawkes was a real person who was convicted of complicity in a plot to blow up the Parliament House in 1605 and was hanged for it along with fellow conspirators. Since 1607, when the failure of the Gun- powder Plot was first commemorated at Bristol, November 5 has been Guy Fawkes Day in England, celebrated with the making of effigies called guys, which are burned in huge bonfires on the evening of that day (see the beginning of Hardy's *Return of the Native*). The guys and bonfires are constant features of the festival; otherwise each English town has its own way of observing the day. Frequent are fireworks, bell-ringing, making and eating of "tharf-cakes" and "Parkin cakes," shouting and chanting of rhymes, and certain pranks associated elsewhere (and in England, too) with Hallowe'en: the wearing of grotesque masks and costumes, taking of gates and fences (sometimes burnt in the bonfires), breaking of windows, and "trick or treat."[36] Obviously this patriotic festival has taken over the rites and customs of older religious festivals, celebrated around the same time of year. Raglan informs us that "The fifth of November was the date of an ancient fire festival," and supposes that once the burning of a human victim was an important feature of it. In so speculating, Raglan ignores the simpler explanation that a people familiar with burning as a means of execution may find it appropriate to burn a criminal's effigy. To this simpler explanation Raglan may object (and he does point out) that Fawkes was not burned but hanged. Yet the hanging of effigies is also a well-known feature of harvest and other festivals.[37] The burning, after all, disposes of the guys.

After mentioning the true manner of Fawkes's execution, Raglan says, rather

---

[35] We should notice too that Becket and Fawkes represent the same cause, that of the Catholic Church against the English king. We can understand fairly well why the slain Becket, in the twelfth century, became a saint and martyr, whereas the executed Fawkes and fellow-conspirators, in the seventeenth century, acquired an odious memory. Yet, though the demonic Fawkes is a Protestant creation (notice also Protestant hostility to Becket's memory beginning with Henry VIII), Catholics have never, so far as I know, remotely considered Fawkes or any other conspira- tor a candidate for sainthood; there have been at most attempts to clear his name and to debunk the Gunpowder Plot (see H. Ross Williamson, *The Gunpowder Plot* [London: Faber, 1951]). One of the executed, Father Garnet, whose guilt may be open to question, appears to have started on Becket's road, for his execution was immediately followed by a miracle: his blood on a straw which fell from the scaffold showed the outline of a face; in due time this became Garnet's face under "a martyr's crown and with the sign of the Cross on his forehead"; prints of the straw were thereafter sold on the continent (see Williamson, pp. 242–243). Worth study is why Fawkes be- came the arch-villian rather than Catesby, Winter, or some other.

[36] See Wright and Lones, *op. cit.*, pp. 145–156.

[37] On rites of burning or hanging effigies, see Frazer, 1911*b*: 220–233 and *Adonis Attis Osiris*, 3d ed. (*Golden Bough* IV [London: Macmillan, 1914]), I, pp. 288–297.

oddly for his general thesis, "but his story has nevertheless been adopted as the myth of this ritual" (1955:76). He now wants to take the true and unchanged historical narrative as the "myth" of the November 5 rituals. He would rather allow a myth to be a true story than to be distorted history. And yet a distorted tradition that Fawkes was burned has really become the popular "myth" of the November 5 festivities. Here is unquetsionably a real person who has become a figure of myth and who has also become an object of apotropaic rites (which bear little resemblance to the Fawkes story, true or distorted). Again what Raglan and Hyman say cannot happen has happened. They must grant the reality of Guy Fawkes, but we know very well that, if we had no record of the Gunpowder Plot, they would point to ancient fire festivals at harvest time, to the burning and hanging of effigies, and flatly deny that Fawkes could possibly be anything but an old deity (a harvest spirit in fox form, no doubt), and that the Gunpowder Plot could be anything but an ancient myth derived from the sacrifice of the divine king.[38] It would be perfectly obvious to them: here was an agent of the current Antichrist (Old Year, Winter, Drought, Death, Evil, ultimately the slain king), just about to kill the king (Christ's viceroy) and lords (and early in the new king's reign too), whom the king's officers rescued in the nick of time by capturing and killing the enemy for the good of the whole kingdom. They would point for confirmation to the record of a Guy Fawkes Day procession: a wagon carried an enthroned image of the Pope, behind which stood a person dressed as Satan, the Pope's privy-councillor, who caressed the effigy and gave advice to it, now in whispers, now in loud tones.[39] Yes, perfectly obvious, but quite wrong.

RAGLAN'S EUHEMERISM

Many more instances of real men who have become subjects of myth and objects of cult or apotropaic rites can be found. Such apotheosis, of course, does not justify us in finding a real person behind Zeus or Odin, or an historical event behind Thor's visit to Jötunheim. That is, we cannot accept either Euhemerism or Raglanism as a satisfactory theory of the origin of the concept of deity or of the origin of myths. I have said "Euhemerism or Raglanism," and Raglan would approve the disjunction, since he considers his ritual theory to be the polar opposite of Euhemerism. But is it? Our treatment of Becket and Fawkes warrants a discussion of Euhemerism, since the subject has provoked many misconceptions.

Although Raglan and Hyman have talked a good deal about Euhemerism and have made "Euhemerist" a term of reproach, they are not clear about what Euhemerism means and do not realize that Euhemerism is not inconsistent with a ritual theory of god and myth origins. According to Raglan, who consulted Smith's *Classical Dictionary* and Hastings' *Encyclopedia,* Euhemerism is the theory that the gods were originally kings and great men who received worship after their deaths (*H* xviii, *OR* 80). Raglan seizes upon the phrase "after death," supposing that the essence of Euhemerism is the worship of a dead king or benefactor. He

[38] In his criticism of Frazer's theory Alfred C. Lyall, pointing to the rituals of Guy Fawkes and to those of Hasan and Hosein among the Shiite Moslems, says, "These and many other such ceremonies are only saved from annexation to mythologic cloudland by lying within the region of accepted history; while all that are found beyond that pale seem to be treated as fair prize by victorious analysis; . . . ," *Asiatic Studies Religious and Social,* 2d ed., II (London: Murray, 1907), p. 209.

[39] See W. Carew Hazlitt, *Faiths and Folklore* (London: Reeves & Turner, 1905), p. 232.

has fallen into a common misconception of Euhemerism; for Euhemeros did *not* say that the first gods were dead kings: he said that they were *living* kings. Raglan and Hyman have not looked up Euhemeros' *Sacred History* to find out what it actually said. The book itself is lost, but Diodoros' history has a summary of it (5.41–46, 6.1). It was the story of an imaginary journey across the Indian Ocean to the Utopian land of Panchaia. There, says Euhemeros, he read an inscription, which informed him that Kronos and Zeus had been kings on earth; and while he was king, "Zeus received honor among all peoples and was called god (*theos*)" (Diod. 6. 1. 10). Euhemeros also tells us that "Others became gods on earth, who because of their benefactions to men won immortal honor and glory" (Diod. 6. 1. 2). That is, Zeus and other men became gods *while they lived on earth*. And this turns out to be a simpler form of Raglan's own theory. For Raglan, like Euhemeros, maintains that the first gods were living kings: "If [my] view is correct, then it follows that the earliest gods were not invisible beings, but men" (*OR* 73); " . . . from the divine king arose in course of time the idea of the god" (*OR* 70). Euhemeros differs from Raglan only in believing that a king named Zeus became the god so named; Raglan, somewhat less naively, believes that the god is the apotheosized kingship, and that the god's name is not necessarily that of any actual king. Raglan reveals his own Euhemerism when he asserts that "invisible gods are the spirits of dead men; not, as the Euhemerists believe, of individual dead men, but of royal dynasties."[40] He is here very careless in expression, since he objects to others' speaking of gods as deified dead men; but he is really making a distinction between ancient and modern Euhemerism. In essence Euhemerism is the statement that gods developed from men who are now dead, and that is Raglan's position: "The king is worshipped when alive; he continues to be wor-shipped when dead, not because he is dead, but because he is believed to be in some way alive" (*OR* 80). So says Raglan, and all Euhemerists agree with him, even those who believe that the first gods were dead kings (for Raglan, after all, the first gods were dying kings).

In Raglan's eyes the arch-Euhemerist was William Ridgeway, who found the origins of drama in the worship of the dead, that is, in the cults of heroes and ancestors.[41] Ridgeway also thought that some gods and heroes had been real persons. What Raglan and Hyman fail to realize is that Ridgeway's theory is as much a theory of ritual origins as their own. Ridgeway said that "solemn songs and dances were part of the propitiatory rites performed at the tombs of heroes in order that they might protect their people, and that the earth, through their kindly interposition, might bring forth her fruits" (1910:108). He further said

---

[40] *OR* 90. According to Raglan (*OR* 73), we should expect the earliest gods to be men and not invisible beings, "for if gods had been thought of from the beginning as spiritual and invisible, it is difficult to imagine how people could have come to believe that a man was a god; the very fact that he was visible would make it obvious that he was not." Raglan takes no notice here of a god's power of taking bodily form or of vanishing as he wishes; but disregarding that omission, we should notice that he spends the next chapter in demonstrating that ghosts, spirits, and gods were always considered material and visible. Then why should the first gods not be a development of visible ghosts? I am not saying that they were; I am only pointing out that Raglan's alternatives are not mutually exclusive. Gods and ghosts are visible if present; but usually they are not present, and so are unseen.

[41] *H* iii, viii, xviii. Hyman (1962a: 242) adopts Raglan's view of Ridgeway. See Ridgeway 1910: chs. i, ii; 1915: sect. i. I see no essential difference between Ridgeway's views and A. B. Cook's, who likewise derived myths from the rites attending dead kings (see note 17 above); yet Raglan and Hyman approve of Cook, who belonged to Jane Harrison's group.

that in Greece and elsewhere such dramatic rites developed into drama: "That a certain ancient ritual can be detected in Greek tragedies I gladly admit, for I have maintained that such there is, and that it arose out of the funeral rites and periodical celebrations to honour the good and noble or to appease the malevolent" (1915:62). True enough, Ridgeway was speaking of the origins of drama; but for Raglan and Hyman the origin of myth and the origin of drama are much the same thing. Hyman, for example, constantly confuses tragic with myth origins. Ridgeway, furthermore, would probably not object to their interpretation of myth as ritual text; he objected only to deriving gods from projections of the rites and worshippers' emotions, to interpreting them as vegetation spirits or seasons, and to tracing all ritual drama back to king sacrifices and combats for the royal succession. Ridgeway was naive in his acceptance of the non-miraculous parts of legend as true history and in his supposing that every god or spirit was directly derived from some once living man who probably bore the same name. The point is that his theory is a ritual theory of myth origin. For there is no incompatibility between Euhemerism, however we define it, and the ritual theory; they are not polar opposites as Raglan and Hyman suppose.[42] Indeed, Raglan's own arguments might support Ridgeway's contention that the legends preserve a fairly accurate record of the actual deeds of men now dead, for Raglan maintains that nothing persists in oral tradition for more than 150 years at most, unless it is ritual-bound: the rituals, periodically reenacted, preserve the oral texts attached to them (*H* i, xi, xiii). If, then, a warrior's deeds were recited at his funeral rites, and if he became a hero or god with a permanent cult (the rites being repeated every year, for example), and if the rites included some mimicry or representation of the deeds, on Raglan's own showing a memory of true historical deeds might be preserved in oral tradition. I do not agree with Ridgeway that legends very often preserve historical fact; and I do not agree with Raglan that only ritual-bound narratives can endure in oral tradition. We know that many folktales have been transmitted over great expanses of space and time without ritual accompaniment, and have suffered only superficial changes in the process. For Raglan, folktales are myths detached from the rituals; but he can hardly deny that they continue to be preserved fairly intact in folk tradition after they have been cut loose from the supposed rituals. In any case, Raglan's and Ridgeway's theories fit nicely together on many points.

So Hyman could very well list Ridgeway in his calendar of ritualist saints rather than in his Euhemerist rogues' gallery.[43] And he could easily place Raglan among the rogues for deriving gods from real kings, which is the Euhemerism of

---

[42] Hyman (1960:127) maintains that the Euhemeristic theory makes myths into "trivial lies," whereas myths embody the "deepest and most profound truths" of a society, expressing "profound sociological and psychological truth." On the contrary, if myths spring from actual events (and I do not say that they do), they would contain some truth; and the theory is that the untruthful parts were not deliberate lies but the result of gradually accumulating errors. As for the profound truths in myths, Hyman and the ritualists never tell us what they are. The statements made in myths are almost without exception factually untrue (a myth might incidentally include a correct geographical or astronomical statement). Any sense in which they might be true is wholly Pickwickian. Truth and falsehood have nothing to do with their value for us: they are good stories.

[43] Among the saints Hyman should also list Robert Graves, who in his *Greek Myths* announces a ritualistic interpretation which centers on matriarchy; but he includes a good deal of "Euhemerism" too.

Euhemeros. Raglan is also guilty of Euhemerism in the broader and looser sense that he and Hyman give to the term: the rationalist interpretation of myth as distorted history. This is Palaiphatism rather than Euhemerism: Palaiphatos' rather absurd *Peri Apistōn* (*On Incredible Tales*) is the principal surviving example of ancient attempts to extract true history from myths by translating mythic into possible events. Raglan too, less naively than Palaiphatos, derives history from myths and traditions. From them, and from no other evidence, as we have seen, he derives a recurring prehistoric (or early historic) event, the annual killing of a king and installation of his successor. And this he does after spending several chapters of *The Hero* in demonstrating that we must not look for any historical truth whatever in legend. To this Raglan would reply that history is what happens once; recurring events are not history—that is, coronations and presidential inaugurations are not history, nor, it seems, are periodic executions, assassinations, and dethronements of kings." Such a distinction will not hold up for a moment; either myth and legend are never veracious in any respect, or they preserve memories of both single and repeated events, if they preserve any at all. The assassination of Becket was not a repeated event.

PREHISTORIC DRAMA

Raglan's theory demands a well developed drama in the ancient Near East, and afterwards in other lands when it had been diffused thence, since he spends several chapters (*H* xx–xxvii) in pointing out the dramatic features of myths: direct discourse, prophecies, agelessness of characters, unities of place and time, and so forth. He is hardly right about all traditional tales, since Peleus, Pelias, Tithonos, and Oedipus grew old, and Greek legendary cycles do not come to an abrupt end, as Raglan maintains. In any case, these features are narrative conventions the world over; that they were originally dramatic conventions and that all narrative arises from drama (as when one person tells another the plot of a play that he has seen) remains for Raglan to demonstrate, especially since the familiar sequence is just the other way: a novel is often dramatized, whereas a play is seldom converted to narrative form (except orally and casually). There is simply no evidence of a well developed drama in the ancient Near East: festival programs and ritual texts survive, but there is nothing truly dramatic in them (the Egyptian coronation drama, as it is called, is in no real sense a drama). We may speak of dramatic rituals, but hardly of ritual dramas in ancient Mesopotamia, Canaan, or Egypt: it is the difference between the Mass and Passion Play. We can agree with Raglan (*H* xxvii) that Athenian tragedy did not suddenly spring into existence in 534 B.C.; nobody, indeed, has said that it did, and there is good evidence for earlier dramatic performances in several parts of Greece (but not very much earlier; was there anything like true drama before 700 B.C.?). Raglan's theory demands dramatic performances all over the Near East at least two thousand years before 600 B.C. Did drama receive a high development in Mesopotamia or Egypt? There is no record of it.

" See *H* xiii; Raglan says "things that happen once only are nothing to the ritualist [meaning the ritual performer]." However, the Gunpowder Plot, the Battle of Kossovo, the American declaration of independence in 1776, the Greek in 1821, are all examples of single events which have meant something to ritual performers. In ancient times single events like victories and foundations of cities gave rise to anniversary festivals.

Let us suppose that Babylon and Egypt had some fine plays which have completely disappeared: why then was Greek drama still primitive and elementary in the sixth century? Raglan, remember, allows no independent starts: all ritual drama and myth were diffused from one center. We find a development of true drama in Greece, India, China, Japan, and late medieval Europe, but hardly anywhere else. True enough, it probably did not have a spontaneous and independent origin in each country; diffusion and cultural influences were at work. But it appeared comparatively late everywhere, and Raglan must have a flourishing drama in the Near East in very early times.

Furthermore is it likely that an elaborate myth-ritual complex could have been transmitted intact from land to land in early times, as Raglan's theory demands? In an essay which surprisingly concludes Hooke's third collection of papers on the Near Eastern myth-ritual pattern (and delivers the *coup de grâce* to the theory built up in all three), S. G. F. Brandon shows that diffusion of such a complex was highly unlikely (Hooke 1958: 261–291); when such a simple device as the winged sun-disk symbol lost its whole significance in its migration from Egypt to Assyria, Persia, and Cappadocia, how can we suppose that the royal sacrificial ritual could preserve not only its whole program but its whole meaning? And who were the carriers? Not even Hooke and his school suppose that this was a proselytizing religion that sent forth missionaries like Christianity and Islam; they allege transmission through trade, war, and colonization. But, asks Brandon, were traders, soldiers, and colonists likely to be interested in spreading this particular cult? Finally he shows that Hooke bases his myth-ritual pattern mainly on the ritual program of the Akitu festival, which was not typical. And I have shown in *Python* (ch. xv) that the Bablyonian myth of beginnings, as told in *Enuma elish,* which was recited at the Akitu festival, was not enacted or symbolized in the ritual program of that festival.

Hocart (1927) has built up a model coronation ritual of 26 parts, which he believes was adapted for use on other solemn occasions, so that other rituals (e.g., marriage and initiation) are derived from it. He explains that "A complete set of all the parts is not known to occur anywhere" (p. 70). The ancient Indian coronation ritual shows 18 parts or component acts, and the Fijian ceremony of installation of a chief shows 17; of the 25 Old World rituals which he analyzes, all others have fewer than 17 of the 26 components. In fact, the Indian coronation ritual, being the only ritual of the 25 that contains as many as 18 of the 26 acts, serves Hocart much as the Akitu ritual serves Hooke. Eleven rituals (44%) have 13 or more component acts (one half or more of the 26); eighteen (72%) have 9 or more (above one-third) ; seven (28%), then, show less than one-third of Hocart's pattern (the Malay marriage ritual has only two components). Component A which is really not an act but a belief (that the king dies and is reborn as a god) appears in 22 rituals, F in 20 ("The King is admonished to rule justly and promises to do so"), E in 19 ("The King must fight a ritual combat [1] by arms, or [2] by ceremonies, and [3] come out victorious"). Only these three components (under one-eighth) appear in more than three-fourths of the rituals; six (under one-fourth) appear in 17 or more (above two-thirds); nine (just above one-third) in 13 or more (above one-half); fifteen (under three-fifths) in 9 or more (above one-third); ten components (nearly two-fifths) , therefore, are seen in fewer than 9 rituals (under one-third), and four of these ten in fewer than 6 rituals: component S (the king takes three steps in imitation of the rising sun) appears in only two and W (vassals and officials are consecrated with the king in either the ceremony or on the subsequent tour) in only one. This hardly looks like a well-established ritual pattern, even if we grant Hocart the validity of his analysis in every instance where he finds a pattern component in a particular ritual (correspondences are sometimes obscure or far-fetched).[45] If his case for a single ritual pattern fails, so must his case for deriving myths from it (Hocart 1952: ch. 1).

CONCLUSION OF CRITIQUE OF RAGLAN'S THEORY

Thus the scholarly foundations of Raglan's theory prove to be weak. William Bascom (1957) has undermined other supports, bringing forward damaging ethnographical and folkloristic facts. He admirably exposes the weaknesses, absurdities, and non-sequiturs of Raglan's arguments that myths must have a ritual origin because they do not have an historical or imaginative origin; that if one part of a legend is certainly unhistorical (as it is bound to be, if we call the story a legend), no part of it can have an historical origin; that no popular story-teller ever invents anything; that if the fairy tales of one country do not have a popular origin in that country (having been borrowed from another country) they do not have a popular origin in any country; and that folktales deal with subjects about which the folk have no knowledge (e.g., royal households).[46] Raglan has put us on our guard about reading history into legends—that is his one sound contribution.

---

[45] Ritual theorists may object that Hocart's case for his ritual pattern is as sound as the case for any myth pattern which scholars have constructed, e.g., the combat-myth pattern which I constructed in *Python* (1959:9–11, 579–583, and tables on pp. 267–273, 359–364). If we make the same statistical analysis of the pattern, which contains 43 themes tabulated for 20 Old World myths, we get the following results. As many as 40 appear in the Python myth as tabulated (and all 43 might be claimed). Seven myths (35%) show 33–40 themes (above three-fourths); eleven (55%) show 29–40 (over two-thirds); fifteen (75%) show 22–40 (over one half); the least number of themes present in any myth is 17 (about 40%). Of the 43 themes, 3 appear in all twenty myths; 20 (nearly one half) in 15–20 myths (at least three-fourths); 22 (a bare majority) in 14–20 (over two-thirds); 30 (about 70%) in 10–20 (at least one half); 41 (95%) in 7–20 (over one-third); the remaining two appear in 6 myths (just under one-third). If one makes this analysis according to the 36 plot-components outlined in *Python* (262–265 and tables on pp. 270, 271, 361) instead of the themes, the results are approximately the same. I would say that this combat-myth pattern is much better established than Hocart's ritual pattern.

[46] The Tory lord speaks often in Raglan's scholarly writing. According to him, only a few human beings are inventive or even intelligent, and they are royalty, nobility, or high clergy; no one else can even repeat anything correctly but must garble it (at the same time, it seems, they must tell a tale always in the same words without variation). I have known a humble miner who composed a ballad with refrain and elementary melody. D. H. Lawrence was fairly inventive in fiction for being the son of a miner. Raglan's upper-class bias appears in his remarks on the story of King Alfred and the cakes. The story cannot be true, he assures us, because "Even if the old woman had dared to whisper it to her cronies, they would not have believed her, and the King would never have recounted a story that would have exposed him to ridicule and lowered the prestige upon which his success depended" (*H* i). But of course the old woman would tell her friends, and they would readily believe her and spread the story; and good King Alfred would certainly tell the story as a joke on himself, since he did not take the kingship as seriously as Lord Raglan does. The story is probably untrue, but not for Raglan's reasons. Likewise Raglan's contention (*H* xi) that nobody who has beliefs about the supernatural can "give free rein to his imagination" concerning his deities, because "the freedom of his imagination must [be] trammelled by the nature of his belief," is not true for ancient Greece or any other land. Raglan is thinking about the Christian creed and the Thirty-Nine Articles; but myths are not creeds, and myth-tellers innovate as they please. Nor is his statement (*H* xi) that an atheist could not tell a myth imaginatively at all sound. Gods may have no existence for an atheist (Raglan's argument), but he knows about the concept of gods, and may hear, enjoy, and even tell myths.

II

HYMAN'S GOODLY THEMIS

WE MUST NOW TURN to Hyman's theory of myth origins. Although Hyman considers Raglan's *The Hero* to be a book of supreme importance in this field and hails Raglan as a confederate, he does not accept the universal slaying of a divine king, does not trace all myths back to a single ritual, and does not rely so heavily on diffusion. His theory is the simple proposition that myths arise only from rituals and from nothing else: every ritual has a spoken or sung accompaniment which is the myth and becomes the traditional tale. He is indebted mainly to Jane Harrison, whose *Themis* has inspired him as no other book: "there are times when I think it is the most revolutionary book of the 20th century," he says in his review of the paperbound *Themis* published in 1962.[1] His admiration of Jane Harrison extends to her whole company—Murray, Cornford, and Cook. This "Cambridge school" was much indebted to Frazer, also a Cambridge man, and *The Golden Bough* is second only to *Themis* in influence on Hyman's ritual theory. Hyman exaggerates the effect which this Cambridge group has had on anthropologists and classicists, for he maintains that their ritual theory of myth has outmoded all other theories.[2] This is far from true, since almost no living mythologist accepts it; and at present the ritual theory has itself become pretty much outmoded by the structural theory of Lévi-Strauss.[3]

HARRISON'S THEORY

Myth for Harrison is "the spoken correlative of things done," the *legomena* which accompany *drōmena*, the rites. Myth and ritual grow up together, two parts of a single whole. In Hyman's words myth is "a spoken correlative that evolves organically out of the acted rite, like a child's patter as he plays."[4] Rites are at first magical in intent and publicly performed, according to Harrison. The partici-

---

[1] Hyman 1962b. He also says, "This theory was of course not new with Miss Harrison; the Greeks knew all about it, . . . " Nowhere in Greek literature do I find the word *mythos* limited to ritual texts, and I cannot even find it employed in that sense. Aristotle uses *mythos* for a dramatic plot (*Poetics* 1450A and *passim*), plainly referring to the legend dramatized. The word employed for ritual speech is *legomena*, as in Paus. 2.37.2. Hyman has relied on Harrison's sentence, "The primary meaning of myth in religion is just the same as in early literature; it is the spoken correlative of the active rite, the thing done; . . . " (1927:328). This is at best misleading. The "early literature" is Homeric epic, in which *ergon* as the antithesis of *mythos* is not ritual action in a single instance. See Fontenrose 1961.

[2] Hyman makes such statements as "Miss Harrison's field of classical studies was overwhelmingly converted to her views, as she notes joyously in the 1927 preface . . . " (1962b:25). This is not only very far from true, since very few classicists were converted, but also a misstatement of her preface: she was happy that W. H. R. Rivers agreed with her on several particulars (p. ix). Rivers was not a classicist, and Harrison made no claim to having influenced him on these matters. She also mentioned (p. vii) Walter Leaf's acceptance of "the Eniautos-Daimon as an integral factor of pre- and post-Homeric religion." Walter Leaf was not the "field of classical studies," and the Eniautos-Daimon is only one of Harrison's views.

[3] See Claude Lévi-Strauss, "The Structural Study of Myth," *Myth: A Symposium*, ed. Thomas Sebeok (Philadelphia: American Folklore Soc., 1955), pp. 50–66, and *Mythologiques: Le cru et le cuit* (Paris: Plon, 1964).

[4] Hyman 1960:126. If so, how do we get the fixed verbal formulae which accompany rituals? Children do not repeat their patter; the same kind of play may produce quite different talk the next day. If ontogeny repeats phylogeny in this respect too (which I am willing to grant), then we should expect the patter to develop into fixed recitations, each accompanying a fixed sequence of acts. But do we find that? May not the child's patter at play repeat early man's patter at work?

pants voice their desires; acting and speaking together, they reach a high pitch of emotion and enthusiasm. The collective emotion is projected or externalized in a person, a *daimōn* or god (Harrison 1927: 16, 45–47, 327–331, 485–490). As Harrison acknowledges in her Introduction (1927: xiii), these collective representations are Durkheim's contribution to her theory, the principal ingredients of which are taken from Durkheim, Bergson, and Frazer.

In this view rite, myth, and god arise and develop together: "[the god's] very existence depends on the ritual that invokes him" (Harrison 1927:10). The words spoken in the rites are the myth, and are imperative, jussive, or optative in mood. But when the meaning of the rites has been forgotten, men find an *aition,* a reason for them in the myth (the *legomena*), which then changes to the indicative mood, becoming a narrative. This narrative is the aetiological myth; Harrison distinguished this from the true myth, which is the sequence of words or story that accompanies rites (and she wished that the word *myth* could be restricted to this sequence). It seems, then, that the story-telling instinct has already been at work: the god, once engendered, must have a life history (a series of *pathē,* according to Harrison).

We may ask how it is possible for the community of worshippers to forget the meaning of the rites, since these carry with them the words which make their intention clear; for the ritualists are always telling us that in rituals the participants must repeat formulae exactly as they have received them, and that for this reason only ritual-bound traditions are likely to be preserved in folk memory. We may also ask whether the words which accompany rites could in most cases suggest the aetiological myth: do mythical narratives so patently show an origin in prayers, hymns of praise, and incantations? We notice too that Harrison invokes a story-telling instinct to help frame the projected god's life-history. This history is also myth in her definition; and so at this point she appears to derive the god from the rites and his myth from instinct.[5] The truth is that Harrison was not so thoroughly a ritualist as Hyman. Later in *Themis* she makes a distinction between ritual myth and heroic legend. In early Greek communities, she says, the deified expression of worshippers' emotions was the Year Spirit (Eniautos Daimōn), perhaps given a different name in each community; he was likely to be identified or merged with either Dionysos or a "saga-hero," as in Athens the old "tribal eponym, Phytalos, fades before the saga-personality Theseus. . . . Theseus, then, the saga-hero, the quasi-historical personality, took on the life-history, the year-history of a fertility-*daimon,* . . ." (1927:327). And so, as Harrison saw it, the Greek drama received its forms from "the old daimonic, magical ritual," its content from the Homeric and other legends (1927:339). Hyman will never allow this distinction (nor Raglan either). He will turn to Harrison's confederate, Gilbert Murray (Excursus in Harrison 1927:341–363), for a demonstration that each hero's passion, as portrayed in tragedy, is cut to the pattern of "the Eniautos myth" and is a sequence of *agōn, pathos, angelos, thrēnos, anagnorisis, theophaneia* —the hero, then, is just a developed, personalized, and historicized Year Spirit.

Harrison's myth-ritual theory obviously agrees on many points with Raglan's.

---

[5] Harrison: 1927:47, "This process of projection, of deification, is much helped by what we may perhaps call the story-telling instinct. The god like his worshipper must have a life-history."

For both, myths and gods are expressions of the rites; and Harrison's Year Spirit who dies and revives every year (and who may become Old Year, who is slain, and New Year, who succeeds him) may be realized in or enacted by a divine king. The great difference is that Raglan is a thorough-going diffusionist who traces all rites and myths back to a single source. For Harrison and Hyman (if I understand them rightly), although there may be diffusion of particular patterns of ritual and myth, the collective emotion of any community, as Durkheim's theory suggests, may produce ritual and therefore myth. Rites, and only rites, have a myth-engendering power, according to Hyman; and, like Raglan, he subsumes all folk narratives under that term. So, as he sees it, again and again, in all parts of the world and in all times, rites have come into being, producing deities and myths in the process. In his most incautious statements he too denies that any element in a myth or other traditional story can be derived directly from experience, dreams, or fantasy: every bit represents something in the parent ritual. For example, if one suggests that maritime peoples modelled many-armed monsters on the octopus, Hyman objects, apparently on the ground that such mythical figures are derived from maskers grotesquely dressed. We may ask what suggests the many-armed ritual figures. In Hyman's own theory they might be engaged in magical rites for the increase of cephalopods; and so a real octopus would suggest the mythical monster after all. To take another example, if one believes that the wars of myth and legend reflect men's experience of wars, Hyman insists instead that they are reflections of ritual combats and sham battles. What put the idea of combat into the rituals? Hyman appears to believe that ritual features are in some way an expression of community experience; but he does not believe that experience can contribute features directly to traditional tales, even when these are told independently of ritual. If he should grant that any feature or episode of a known myth or legend has come to it directly from experience, even after it is no longer attached to a ritual (and we generally encounter myths when they are not ritual-bound), his whole case for ritual origin is weakened: for we may then ask why any portion of the narrative must have a ritual origin. Today we observe that stories, oral or written, are derived directly from experience—from events, dreams, fantasies, and imagination working on experience. In fact, present-day rituals contribute almost nothing to fiction. Although Hyman believes that the basic pattern of all imaginative literature goes back to ancient myth-ritual patterns, he cannot deny that the superstructure is mainly otherwise derived. That is, fictional episodes are drawn directly from life without having to pass through a filter of ritual enactment. Why should this not be true of traditional tales in early times and in primitive communities?[6]

---

[6] Of course, as Raglan (*H* xii) grants, the imagination can work only with materials known to the imaginer; but Raglan uses this truism in an attempt to prove that common people cannot invent folktales, since many tales have such subjects as kings, nobles, palaces, and the like. He and Hyman consider Euhemeristic any suggestion that features of a traditional story came directly from experience by way of the imagination working on it rather than from ritual. Yet they recognize that novels contain episodes and characters suggested by real events and persons without being attempts to narrate true happenings or depict real persons. But why grant this for written fiction and not for traditional tales, since the ritualists' methods of analysis and interpretation can (and do) as easily reduce a novel to the myth-ritual pattern (compare Weisinger's treatment of Shakespeare discussed at the end of this chapter)? For example, a ritualist analysis (which I do not recommend) of *Pickwick Papers* may be made as follows. Mr. Pickwick, incarcerated in a

THE PALAIKASTRO HYMN

Since Hyman relies on Harrison much as Raglan relies on Frazer, we must consider the concrete evidence on which Harrison built her theory, just as we examined Frazer's foundations. She must be able to show ritual *legomena* (the real myth in her definition) in the act of becoming aetiological myth (myth as we know it, the story told independently of rites). She believed that she had found this in the "Hymn of the Kouretes," inscribed on a stone which the British School's excavations uncovered at Palaikastro, Crete, in 1904.[7] Part of the text has disappeared, but the remainder shows plainly a hymn sung in the worship of Zeus at Heleia on the eastern edge of the island. The worshippers invoke Zeus as *megistos kouros Kroneios*, bidding him come to Dikte for the year (ἐς ἐνιαυτόν) and rejoice in the song which they sing at his altar; for it was there (they sing) that the shield-bearing Kouretes received the Zeus-babe from Rea and concealed him (some words have disappeared, and the name *Kouretes* is not visible). After a break in the text of one couplet and refrain the singers mention blessings (presumably attendant on the rescue of Zeus and his accession to power): the Seasons (*Hōrai*, but here some of the text is gone, so that we cannot be completely sure of the Seasons), Justice (*Dika*), and wealth-loving Peace (*philolbos Eirēna*). Finally the singers summon the god to come leaping to their farms and cities (θόρ' ἐς ποίμνια,...). Harrison translated this conclusion as follows: "To us also leap for full jars, and leap for fleecy flocks, and leap for fields of fruit, and for hives to bring increase.... Leap for our Cities, and leap for our sea-borne ships, and leap for our young citizens and for goodly Themis" (1927:8). The translation is in part conjectural, since there are several gaps in the text. If we accept Diehl's and Guarducci's text (which is later than that which Harrison used), "To us" must be stricken, the "full jars" become herds of cattle, the "hives" become houses, and Themis is renowned (κληνάν) rather than goodly (καλάν). Harrison's translation of the preposition *es* as "for" is misleading: a reader is bound to understand "for" in "leap for fleecy flocks" as "for the sake of," i.e., for their increase and welfare, and that is the way Hyman has understood it. It is true that *es* sometimes may be expressed as "for" in an English translation, but only in the proper context. Its primary meaning is *into,* and after a verb of motion like θρώσκειν it can be understood only as *into* or *to.*[8] So the singers bid Zeus come leaping (rushing, running) at the New Year to the herds, flocks, fields, houses, cities, ships, citizens, and Themis. Harrison's translation slants the hymn's meaning to her interpretation.

---

debtors' prison is the divine king going to his death in "the pit" (and does not the Fleet prison suggest the deep as a death realm?); Mr. Pickwick emerging from prison is the resurrected king, renewed and purified. One should observe that Mr. Pickwick was the eponymous founder (culture hero-god) and General Chairman (king) of the Pickwick Club, where he had (verbal) combat with the obnoxious Mr. Blotton (the Antagonist). In his very first sentence, moreover, Dickens introduces his hero as "the immortal Pickwick," surely a divine king. A ritual theorist may conclude that the tale descends directly from prehistoric rituals—more plainly than does *Origin of Species,* where Hyman finds the myth-ritual pattern.

[7] Harrison 1927: ch. i; see p. 1, "It lets us see myth as well as ritual in the making, . . . " For the text of the Palaikastro Hymn, see Appendix.

[8] See Nilsson 1950:550 and Willetts 1962: 214. Nilsson believes that the verb, in addition to its literal meaning of "leap," connotes "mount," as in animal sexual union; thus the worshipers invite Zeus to inject fertility into the herds, flocks, cities, and citizens. Guarducci (1939: 17–18) wants to interpret "leap" metaphorically, but in the usual meaning of the verb.

In this hymn Harrison saw "myth as well as ritual in the making"; it was proof of her thesis. The singers, who dance as they sing, as she interpreted the hymn, are young men, *Kouroi* or *Kourētes;* their (or their ancestors') dance began as a magical ritual for the increase of cattle and crops; out of themselves, their collective emotion, they projected a great Kouros, and to him their song is addressed; thus are *daimones* born. The leader of the chorus may represent the Kouros on each ritual occasion. The song is the true myth, the *legomena* which accompany the ritual, and it is mainly in the imperative mood. The worshippers bid the Kouros come and do exactly as they do; he leaps and dances with them. Gradually the Kouros was fitted with a life history, which, finally severed from the rituals and orally transmitted in prose (which nearly everybody speaks), became an aetiological myth, told in the indicative mood: what the god was once told to do he was now said to have done. So from out of the hymn which the Kouretes sang in the Cretan rites of the Kouros came that myth of Zeus' birth which we read in Hesiod's *Theogony* and Apollodoros' *Library*. Such is Harrison's interpretation.

If she was right, we have a myth in embryo, in primitive form, almost literally a fossil in its inscribed state. But is this hymn so primitive as all that? The inscription is dated around A.D. 200 or later. The poem is admittedly earlier but, to judge from its style and form, cannot be much if at all earlier than 300 B.C. This Harrison granted. She insisted, however, that it contains "primaeval" material, which cannot be dated because it is *nomimon*. She pointed to the antiquity in Crete of the cult of Zeus Diktaios, presumably the Zeus of the hymn, who is bid come to Dikte; and we know from inscriptions and Strabo (10.4.6, p. 475) that the Eteocretans maintained the cult of Zeus Diktaios. Heleia (Palaikastro) was an Eteocretan city, and archaeological finds, dating from the seventh to fifth centuries B.C., indicate a sanctuary of some importance at that time; and since the hymn inscription was found near the temple site, archaeologists and other scholars are fairly certain that this was the sanctuary of Zeus Diktaios. Harrison believed that the Palaikastro hymn faithfully repeats in later metrical form the primitive content of earlier hymns. As she saw it, the hymn has three parts:

First we have in the refrain the actual invocation; the god is addressed by his various titles and instructed how, where and when to come— . . . .

Next by an easy transition we have a statement of the ritual performed. The god is adjured to rejoice in the dance and song which the worshippers make to him . . . The reason, or rather the occasion, of this dance and song is next stated. We have in fact what would usually be called an 'aetiological' myth. The worshippers dance round the altar of the Kouros because 'here the shielded Nurturers took the Kouros, an immortal child from Rhea, and with noise of beating feet hid him away.'

Next follows a lamentable gap. When the text re-emerges we are midway in the third factor, the statement of the benefits which resulted from the events recounted in the myth, benefits which clearly it is expected will be renewed in the annual restatement and ritual re-enactment of this myth. The coming Seasons are to be fruitful, Dikè is to possess mankind, the Kouros by leaping in conjunction with his worshippers is to bring fertility for flocks and fields, prosperity to cities and sea-borne ships, and young citizens. (Harrison 1927:9–10)

It was Harrison and Murray who called this the Hymn of the Kouretes. Her theory requires that the singers represent the Kouretes and that they dance while they sing, ostensibly in imitation of the mythical Kouretes' dance around the infant Zeus, but in reality repeating the ancient magical ritual out of which the myth took shape. With such conviction did she state her interpretation in *Themis* that many scholars have accepted her title and have without question considered that the singers represented Kouretes. Yet the careful reader will find nothing in the hymn to show either that the singers considered themselves to be Kouretes or that they danced. In fact, they say plainly that they are not dancing, καὶ στάντες ἀείδομεν τεὸν ἀμφὶ βωμὸν εὐερκῆ (5): they sing standing about the altar, having at the outset taken their position there. Harrison gets around this difficulty by interpreting, " ' . . . they come to a stand at his well-fenced altar.' We have clearly a ritual dance accompanying a song." We clearly have nothing of the sort. Furthermore the singers make music on lyres and flutes.⁹ If they are enacting the role of Kouretes, they should be beating with spears and swords on shields as they dance, for that is the myth as the Greeks told it.¹⁰ If the invoked *kouros* is Zeus, he should be the Zeus-babe around whom the Kouretes danced. But Harrison would not allow that: she believed that *kouros* could mean only a full-grown youth, the projection of the dancing youths called Kouretes. She takes μέγιστε κοῦρε of the invocation as "greatest of grown-up youths," "Full-grown Youth" (1927:11). This might seem to work against her theory of the myth-ritual relation. But in the Kouretes' dance she sees "a rite of mimic death and resurrection practised at a ceremony of initiation" (1927:27). A mimic rebirth, therefore, could put the infant Zeus into the myth.

Harrison's surprise at finding Zeus a teen-age youth, when he was always an adult or babe in literature, set her on the Durkheimian path to her myth-ritual theory. Contrary to her assertion, however, that *kouros* cannot mean *son* or *child* and cannot connote a relationship to a parent, the word is poetically used in these senses as early as the Homeric epics (in a footnote Harrison grants that *kouros* may be a "rough equivalent" of *pais* or *huios*). It even refers to an unborn man-child in Iliad 6.59, ὅντινα γαστέρι μήτηρ / κοῦρον ἐόντα φέροι. In Odyssey 19.523 κοῦρον Ζήθοιο ἄνακτος means "son of King Zethos" and in Sophocles' *Philoktetes* 562 οἵ τε Θησέως κόροι means "the sons of Theseus" as full-grown men. Thus the word may connote kinship, as in English "John's boys" means "John's sons" of any age. Furthermore a *kourotrophos* is not a nurse of grown boys (as Harrison recognized when she discussed the goddess Kourotrophos in her *Prolegomena to the Study of Greek Religion*). Once we realize that *kouros* may mean *son* or *man-child*, we perceive that the singers do not call on Zeus Kouros, who is then designated Kroneios ("Cronian," adjective for genitive), as Harrison supposed, but on *kouros Kroneios*, the Cronian boy (same as *Kronios pais*, son of Kronos).¹¹ So *kouros* has

---

⁹ ὑπακτίσι μείξαντες ἅμ' αὐλοῖσιν. The first word may mean either pipes or harps. Harrison and Willetts take it to mean stringed instruments, but it may be either a kind of reed instrument different from *auloi* or a modifier of αὐλοῖσιν.

¹⁰ Apollod. 1. 1. 7. Nilsson (1950:547) also points out that the singers do not present themselves as Kouretes and do not dance: "The singers . . . are an ordinary sacred chorus which sings the hymn standing around the altar. . . . The words in which this is said cannot be misunderstood, . . . " Yet he grants an association of the singers with Kouretes and interprets *megistos kouros* in Harrison's fashion. Guarducci (1939:13–14) rejects the interpretation of the singers as dancing Kouretes.

¹¹ See Guarducci 1939: 10–11.

no reference to Zeus as youth, nor even to the Zeus-babe, who is mentioned only in the singers' reason for calling Zeus to Dikte:

> ἔνθα γάρ σε παῖδ' ἄμβροτον ἀσπί[δεσσι Κούρητες]
> πὰρ 'Ρέας λαβόντες πόδα κ[υκλῶντες ἀπέκρυψαν.]

"For here Kouretes received thee, an immortal child, from Rea and with encircling step concealed thee with shields." That is where the Zeus-child was born; what more appropriate than that he favor his birthplace with his benevolent presence? We should notice that the word *Kourētes* is restored in this stanza: it appears nowhere in the visible text, and, in fact, Harrison read *trophēes* "Nurturers" instead in this place. If the restoration is right, the singers were obviously not referring to themselves as Kouretes, but to the Kouretes' role in the myth; they referred to them in the third person as different from themselves.

But did the singers refer to themselves in the refrain when they sang βέβακες δαιμόνων ἀγώμενος? That is, did they represent the band of *daimones* called Kouretes, whose leader was *megistos kouros* Zeus? Harrison (accepting Murray's rendering) translated "thou art come at the head of thy Daimones" (1927:7). Willetts has "Here now present, leading thy Spirits" (1962:212). But should not these words mean "You stand (hold the office of) ruler of gods"; that is, "you are ruler of gods"? This is the common meaning of the perfect of *bainein;* furthermore the above translations have Zeus present at the outset before the singers summon him to come. As early as the Homeric epics, *daimones* is a synonym of *theoi;* and the participle ἡγούμενος (Attic form) as a noun meaning "ruler," "governor," "commander," is common enough.[12] Moreover the genitive δαιμόνων confirms my interpretation; for when this verb means "rule" it governs the genitive, and when it means "lead" it governs the dative.

The singers summon Zeus to Dikte, the name of a mountain. It is uncertain what mountain Dikte is. Harrison identified it with Hesiod's Aigaion, some fifty miles from Heleia; the distance caused her some difficulty, which she overcame by pointing to the long-established cult of Zeus Diktaios among the Eteocretans of eastern Crete. She would have welcomed the later conclusions of Nilsson, Guarducci, and others that Dikte is a mountain near Heleia. The truth may be that several mountains in Crete were called Dikte; certainly more than one was the reputed birthplace of Zeus (one was Ida).[13] We should notice that Zeus is never addressed as Diktaios in the hymn; he is only summoned to Dikte. There is nothing beside the site of the inscription to show that the hymn was an Eteocretan com-

---

[12] See Herod. 9. 1. 1, Aesch. *Ag.* 1363, Soph. *Phil.* 386, for the meaning "ruler." The word is used of a Roman governor in Lucian *Alex.* 44; in Christian Greece it has meant "abbot." See the Dionysiac hymn in Soph. *Ant.* 1115–1121: invocation of the god is followed by announcement of his rulership, "(you) who rule in the vales of Eleusinian Deo."

[13] On Dikte, see Harrison 1927: 2–5; Nilsson 1950: 458–460; Guarducci 1939: 3–7; Willetts 1962: 215–216. Hesiod mentions Lyktos and Mt. Aigaion (*Theog.* 477–484), modern Lasithi. The notion (see Willetts, *loc. cit.*) that Hesiod has Uranos and Gaia send Rea to Lyktos, where she bore her son, whom Gaia then received and carried first to Lyktos (where he already was) and then to a cave on Mt. Aigaion seems to me to be a misinterpretation of the passage and not to make sense. τὸν μέν οἱ ἐδέξατο γαῖα πελώρη / Κρήτῃ ἐν εὐρείῃ τραφέμεν ἀτιταλλέμεναί τε (*Theog.* 479–480), simply means that Rea bore her son on the Cretan earth, where he would grow up; here γαῖα has its common meaning. Then Rea is subject of ἷκτο φέρουσα (481), and this sentence (481–482) explicates the preceding (479–480). Rea is also subject of κρύψεν (482) and ἐγγυάλιξεν (485; would not Kronos be suspicious if Gaia rather than Rea came to deliver the new-born babe to him?).

position specifically designed for the Zeus cult of Heleia. It may be a hymn sung throughout Crete, written by a late fourth-century poet to celebrate the Cretan Zeus, born and concealed in a cave on a Cretan mountain. The mythical *aition* of the song, on which Harrison laid great stress, is simply this well-known birth; it is mentioned only in one clause (which occupies two verses, the second stanza), introduced by γάρ, which subordinates it to the summons of the refrain; and the clause merely states the reason for calling Zeus to Dikte. As for the "statement of the ritual performed," of which this myth is the "reason, or rather the occasion," nothing is mentioned but singing around an altar to musical accompaniment.

For the myth, so briefly mentioned, the poet was probably more dependent on Hesiod's *Theogony* than on ancient cult traditions of Crete. In both *Theogony* and the hymn, Rea left the Zeus-child to be nurtured in Crete, the child was concealed, and the event finally produced the Horai (Seasons), who include Justice and Peace. This last statement (the fourth stanza) was obviously suggested by *Theogony* 901–902: Zeus married Themis, who bore him the Horai, who are Eunomia (Good Order), Justice, and Peace. Eunomia is omitted in the hymn, but the others are mentioned in Hesiod's order. And the naming of the daughters of Zeus and Themis determined the final phrase of the final stanza, "and leap to renowned Themis": the god must visit Themis again to renew the blessings of justice, peace, and order. Only the hymn's reference to the Kouretes as the Zeus-child's receivers (if the restoration is correct) is not derived from the *Theogony*. Hesiod, however, knew about the dancing Kouretes (fr. 198 Rzach), and that feature of the myth was obviously established in tradition and poetry long before 300 B.C.[14]

To sum up: the hymn-singers were not dancers, did not represent Kouretes, and did not project a "Greatest Kouros" to be their leader. They did not conceive Zeus as leader of a *thiasos* of *daimones,* the Kouretes of myth and cult. They bade Zeus come to Dikte and bless the Cretan land.[15] The hymn echoes Hesiod's *Theogony* and is composed in highly developed rhythm and form, which are anything but primitive.

As a *hymnos klētikos* (invocatory hymn), this hymn manifests all the conventions of *hymnoi klētikoi,* as Harrison tells us, calling it "a Hymn of Invocation of a ritual type fairly well known" (1927:9), like the Dionysiac hymn of the Elean women, the Dionysiac hymn of Philodamos, and some choruses of tragedy.[16] We should not, however, see in these hymns the survival of some primitive ritual form, but an advanced poetic genre. The summoning of the god to the city or land of the hymn singers, the blessings that he is asked to confer, allusion to a myth which connects him with the place, the singers' reference to their song and its music, the refrain—these features we find in each. We should also notice that the language of the hymn is Doric literary *koinē* and not the local dialect of Eteocretans.

---

[14] See Eur. *Bacch.* 120–129.

[15] After my own reading and study of the poem, resulting in the interpretation which I here express, I found much of it confirmed by Nilsson and Guarducci (see notes 10, 11); both still believe, however, that Zeus leads a band of *daimones* to Dikte and do not notice the poet's dependence on Hesiod. On the language as common Doric without trace of local Cretan dialect see Guarducci (1939: 8). The hymn is relatively late and highly sophisticated poetry.

[16] Elean hymn: Plut. *Mor.* 299B. Philodamos' hymn: Diehl, *Anth. Lyr. Gr.* II, 252–256. Delphic hymns: *Fouilles de Delphes* 3.2.137, 138. Tragic choruses: e.g., Soph. *Ant.* 1115–1154, Eur. *Bacch.* 977–1023.

So, properly interpreted, the Palaikastro hymn does not support Harrison's theory; it is not the firm foundation that she wanted it to be. It did not arise from the patter which accompanied the original ritual of Zeus Diktaios or Zeus Kouros; it is not "the spoken correlative of the acted rite" (Harrison 1927:328). Harrison's whole interpretation of the hymn as showing the projection of the god from the worshippers' emotions is imposed upon and read into a late classical composition.

We need not go farther into *Themis* to demonstrate the weakness of Harrison's interpretation when she deals with Oschophoria, Bouphonia, and other festivals (granted that the book has great merits, is pleasant reading, and is sound in many particulars). Her *Eniautos Daimōn* is an imaginative figment: the phrase is never found in ancient Greek literature or inscriptions; and, in fact, the combination is impossible, since *eniautos* is not an adjective (an ἐνιαύσιος δαίμων or ὁ δαίμων 'Ενιαυτός is possible, but unattested; the rarely personified *Eniautos* is the nearest that can be found).

CONCLUSION OF CRITIQUE OF HYMAN'S THEORY

At times Hyman expresses agreement with Harrison's dictum that the term "myth" should be restricted to a ritual-bound tale or to a tale which has a ritual origin. This definition implies that there are other kinds of traditional narrative, but, like Raglan, Hyman is inclined to find a mythical (and therefore ritual) origin for almost everything in folklore, literature, and art. His definition of myth becomes wide enough to include everything that anyone has ever called myth—indeed all speech threatens to become myth in Hyman's recent writings. Yet if we define myth as all speech, does not *myth* become zero, a constant factor, in our studies of folklore and literature? To say that a story is a myth would be no more than to say that it is composed of words, and we would be saying nothing of significance; we would simply need another term to distinguish the traditional narratives from other modes of verbal expression.

Hyman goes so far as to reduce scientific and scholarly writings to myth. In *The Tangled Bank* he "[relied heavily] on the ritual theory of Jane Harrison and Gilbert Murray."[17] He tells us that the *Origin of Species* shows "the basic ritual stages of tragedy" (1962a: 28) as outlined by Murray: the struggle for existence corresponds to *agōn* and *sparagmos,* survival of the fittest to *anagnorisis* and *epiphany.* Darwin, of course, could hardly have read *Themis* or Murray's "Excursus" included in it. What Hyman means is that all imaginative constructions of the human mind are bound to fall into this pattern. Even if Hyman's theory were valid, would it tell us anything at all? The basic myth-ritual pattern becomes simply a synonym of plot or structure. Hyman's method in criticism is very much *a priori.*

Disciples are always likely to outdo the master, as in the first chapter of Chesterton's *The Napoleon of Notting Hill,* where each contemporary movement produced an enthusiastic advocate who carried the doctrine to its extreme logical consequences—e.g., the vegetarian movement produced a man who objected to eating plants, too, refusing to shed "the green blood of the silent animals" and advocating that men's diet be limited to salt. Thus does Herbert Weisinger, Hyman's disciple,

---

[17] 1962a: ix. See my review, Fontenrose 1962.

apply the myth-ritual pattern to Shakespeare's tragedies.[18] From Murray, Hooke, and Raglan he constructs a pattern of nine constituent parts. Four of the nine, however, have disappeared long since and are not present in Shakespearean tragedy; two are there only by implication (indispensable role of the divine king and settling of destinies). So only three are left: combat, suffering, and resurrection. Now the tragic hero obviously has no resurrection: Hamlet or Othello or Macbeth seems pretty well done for at the play's end. Weisinger deals easily with that difficulty: "the real protagonist of tragedy is the order of God against which the tragic hero has rebelled"; the protagonist has made the mistake of merging himself with the antagonist "into a single challenge against the order of God." So Weisinger finds *Othello* (though not perfect) to be Shakespeare's best tragedy, because it comes nearest to fulfilling the requirements of the truncated "pattern"; ". . . the myth and ritual elements have not been assimilated into [*Hamlet*]," which has a faulty ending. *Lear* is even more faulty, because Shakespeare put Lear's "moment of illumination" in the wrong place and mishandled the settling of destinies. And *Macbeth* "is a tale signifying nothing." Shakespeare's other tragedies are complete failures (so Weisinger informs us); not one, not even *Othello,* is a "successful" tragedy, because poor Will failed to construct his plays on the one correct pattern.[19] This is not an unfair example of the myth-ritual theory as a tool of literary criticism.

---

[18] "The Myth and Ritual Approach to Shakespearean Tragedy," *The Centennial Review,* I (1957), 142–166, and somewhat more soberly in "An Examination of the Myth and Ritual Approach to Shakespeare," in *Myth and Mythmaking,* ed. H. A. Murray (New York: Braziller, 1960), pp. 132–140. See Fontenrose 1962: 77–78 on the prose style of the Hyman school.

[19] In his later essay (see note 18) Weisinger has some qualms about his *Centennial Review* article, attributing its excesses to "the euphoria of conversion"; now, it appears, nobody knows "what the myth and ritual pattern actually is," since no such pattern "exists or ever existed in any real sense; it is a modern, scholarly reconstruction" for ordering diverse materials (that is, it is a tool of *a priori* criticism). He grants that he might have been forcing "a dogmatic shape upon the individual reluctant body for the sake of a general theoretical ideal," so that, he admits, he may have been a little too hard on Shakespeare. Still he believes that his "approach" is sound, if used cautiously, and that any critical system is subject to the same abuses. But have the great critics adhered to a "critical system"?

III

THE KING OF THE WOODS

"THE KEY IMAGE of *The Golden Bough*," Hyman says (1962a:439), "the king who slays the slayer and must himself be slain, corresponds to some universal principle we recognize in life." Perhaps some of us fail to recognize this universal principle, being less perceptive than those who, with Hyman's approval, find it in "Soviet managerial mobility" and the like.[1] Yet here is the springboard of Frazer's theory from which the whole ritualist school ultimately takes off. The slayer is the King of the Woods, *Rex Nemorensis,* attached to Diana's sanctuary at Aricia in the Alban Hills, whom Frazer made a familiar figure, vivid and pitiful—or rather, one may suspect, Frazer created an interesting character and identified him with the King of the Woods. Whether Frazer's character is really the ancient Rex Nemorensis is the question now before us. For in a study of the ritual theory of myth origins we can hardly neglect him. He is not only the occasion of the theory in its early Frazerian form, but also, if Frazer was right, supporting evidence— the one example from classical antiquity of a king (at least of someone who had the title) who was put to death when his strength failed, or, more accurately, whose failing strength and skill allowed another man to put him to death. But was Frazer right about this person? Did he interpret the evidence correctly?

THE GHASTLY PRIEST

As Frazer read the evidence, the priest of Diana Nemorensis at her great sanctuary beside Lake Nemi near Aricia was a runaway slave who had won his office by killing his predecessor. The fugitive had first to pluck a bough from a certain tree in Diana's sacred grove; this gave him the right to challenge and fight the incumbent priest. If he killed the priest, he succeeded to the office and bore the title Rex Nemorensis. But the king had little joy of his office, as Frazer saw him:

> The post which he held by this precarious tenure carried with it the title of king; but surely no crowned head ever lay uneasier, or was visited by more evil dreams, than his. For year in year out, in summer and winter, in fair weather and in foul, he had to keep his lonely watch, and whenever he snatched a troubled slumber it was at the peril of his life. The least relaxation of his vigilance, the smallest abatement of his strength of limb or skill of fence, put him in jeopardy; grey hairs might seal his death-warrant. . . . To gentle and pious pilgrims at the shrine the sight of him might well seem to darken the fair landscape, as when a cloud suddenly blots the sun on a bright day. The dreamy blue of Italian skies, the dappled shade of summer woods, and the sparkle of waves in the sun, can have accorded but ill with that stern and sinister figure. (Frazer 1911a: I, 9)

And so on in Frazer's lush, flowery style.[2] Frazer identified the shorn bough with the golden bough which Aeneas needed for entry into the death realm; he identified the golden bough with mistletoe; and in Diana's grove (likely to be mainly

---

[1] And should one call it an image of *The Golden Bough?* Is it not rather the main subject of discourse of both the first chapter of *The Magic Art* and of several other sections of the whole work?

[2] On Frazer's style see Fontenrose 1962:77. His model was apparently Ruskin. Notice that his first sentence in *The Magic Art* introduces Turner's painting, and his second "the divine mind of Turner" (Frazer 1911a: I, 1).

beeches) he placed that holm oak (*ilex*) from which Aeneas plucked the bough. The King of the Woods represented Virbius (whom the Romans identified with Hippolytos), a subordinate but chief (or only?) male deity at the Arician sanctuary; as Virbius the King was Diana's own consort. Finally, Diana was embodied in the oak on which grew the golden bough.[3]

These identifications were admittedly speculative and have not held up well under criticism. Lang, Conway, and others have pretty well destroyed all links between the Arician bough and Aeneas' golden bough, and between either and mistletoe.[4] Obviously Aeneas did not go all the way from Cumae to the Alban Hills to pluck the golden bough, as even a hasty reading of *Aeneid* 6.133–211 will show. Aeneas plucked the bough in that very forest where the Trojans cut down trees for Misenus' funeral pyre (this alone shows that it could not be Diana's sacred grove), and the tree from which it was taken could not be very far from *fauces grave olentis Averni* (6.201). Aeneas, moreover, was not a runaway slave (although *profugus*); the bough gave him no right to fight anyone for a title (he was already king); it came from a tree sacred to *Juno inferna* (not to Diana); it would be Aeneas' passport to the death realm and a gift to Proserpina (= *Juno inferna*.[5]

What do we really know about the "ghastly priest" at Nemi? Frazer's haunted figure appears to be derived mostly from a sentence of Strabo's, who, speaking of Diana's shrine at Aricia, mentions the barbaric and "Scythian" rite which prevailed there:

καθίσταται γὰρ ἱερεὺς ὁ γενηθεὶς αὐτόχειρ τοῦ ἱερωμένου πρότερον δραπέτης ἀνήρ· ξιφήρης οὖν ἐστιν ἀεὶ περισκοπῶν τὰς ἐπιθέσεις, ἕτοιμος ἀμύνεσθαι. [5.3.12, p. 239: He is appointed priest who, being a runaway slave, has managed to murder the man who was priest before him; he is always armed with a sword, keeping watch for the onsets, ready to defend himself (to ward them off)].

Strabo does not say that he had seen the priest. He speaks only of a sword-bearing man, ready to defend himself against attacks which he expected, presumably from a would-be successor. Frazer inflates this person into a sleepless guardian of a tree:

In the sacred grove there grew a certain tree round which at any time of the day, and probably

---

[3] Frazer 1911a: I, ch. i. See also his *Lectures on the Early History of the Kingship* (London: Macmillan, 1905), ch. i.

[4] Lang 1901: ch. xi; R. S. Conway 1928: ch. iii. The mistletoe, as Lang and others have pointed out, appears only in a simile (*Aen.* 6.205–207), and furthermore Virgil does not say that the golden bough looked like mistletoe. He says only that it gleamed amid the boughs of the *ilex* tree as the yellow flowers of mistletoe appear (they hardly gleam or shine) among the boughs of the host tree; that is, it is not a distinct object which catches the eye at once, and one must look carefully to notice the color almost hidden among leaves and boughs. Conway's study does more damage to Frazer's identifications than does Lang's, who understood Servius' *publica opinio* and *istum inde sumpsit colorem* (on *Aen.* 6.136) much as Frazer had. The former phrase does not mean that the public opinion of Servius' time identified Aeneas' bough with the Arician: it means merely "current report." In the latter phrase *colorem* has no reference to the bough's color, but means "suggestion," as Conway says: the Arician bough suggested a golden bough that Aeneas must pluck for entry to the lower world; for the bough gave Aeneas the right to present a dead man, Misenus, to the underworld powers, so that Aeneas himself, after entering the land of death, might return alive to the upper world. So I understand Servius, and it is a typically Servian interpretation.

[5] As Lang (1901:211) sensibly points out, the golden bough can be plucked only by the destined man; no other man or instrument can sever it. But any man had the strength to pluck the Arician bough, although only a fugitive slave might do so with impunity. Servius (*Aen.* 6.136) appears to say that the Arician bough was a branch of the tree itself, and any branch of that tree; his words give no hint of another meaning.

far into the night, a grim figure might be seen to prowl. In his hand he carried a drawn sword, and he kept peering warily about him as if at every instant he expected to be set upon by an enemy. He was a priest and a murderer; and the man for whom he looked was sooner or later to murder him and hold the priesthood in his stead. (Frazer 1911a: I, 8–9)

But Strabo does not say that the priest guarded a tree. Frazer's tree, of course, is that from which the runaway slave plucked a bough. Only Servius (*Aen.* 6.136) mentions this tree and this bough: *in huius templo . . . fuit arbor quaedam de qua infringi ramum non licebat. dabatur autem fugitivis potestas ut siquis exinde ramum potuisset auferre monomachia cum fugitivo templi sacerdote dimicaret: nam fugitivus illic erat sacerdos . . .* One wonders why the priest had to be so wakeful and on his guard? The breaking of a bough only gave the runaway a right to single combat (*monomachia*) with the incumbent priest. Frazer appears to assume that the man who broke the bough had the right to murder the priest, even in his sleep. But if, as Servius says, the breaking of a bough gave the fugitive only a right to challenge, why could the King of the Woods not relax now and then and go to bed? Frazer might have replied that the priest would want to avoid a combat if he could, especially if he was growing old and weak (yet in that case to be outdoors all a rainy or chill winter's night would hardly be a better choice; and one wonders why the priest did not station subordinates at the tree —this possibility Frazer ignored). But could his constant watch with drawn sword prevent a combat?

Let us review such an occasion as Frazer imagines. In the dead of night the priest with drawn sword faces a fugitive slave, a desperate man, who has come armed with a sword to the tree, intending to break a bough from it. No one else is there (we must suppose that the priest had the place dimly lighted on moonless nights, since the grove would be pitch dark otherwise; yet that light would tell the fugitive where the tree stood). The priest attacks the invader. What will the attacked man do? Will he refuse to defend himself, even though he carries a sword, just because he has not yet broken a bough? Obviously he will defend himself, since his only alternative is to be killed by the priest; if he should retreat and leave the sanctuary, he would risk capture as a fugitive slave. If he kills the priest, he can break a bough and say the next morning that he plucked it first. Can we suppose him an overscrupulous person? Even in broad daylight what would an invading fugitive have to lose by defending himself, if he approached the tree and saw the priest rushing at him with drawn sword? Since death would be the only likely alternative to defense of his person, he would in desperation defend himself, even though the combat might end in his own death, or, if he was victorious, be followed by his execution for killing the priest before he had a right to do so—if that was a rule of the game. The priest, therefore, had a fight on his hands anyway; his constant vigil spared him no combat, even on Frazer's assumptions. Would the priest not realize this? So why stay out all night in rain or frost?

Servius does not say that the priest watched the tree. Strabo says that he was on the watch for *epitheseis,* that is, for onsets or attacks, presumably on his person (but not necessarily), for he was "ready to ward them off." Can we be sure that he had a right to keep a fugitive slave from breaking a bough? Or that the fugitive had no right to defend himself, if the priest attacked him as he approached the

tree?[a] Pausanias sheds no more light on the subject. He mentions the myth according to which Hippolytos came to Aricia after his resurrection and reigned there
as king, dedicating a *temenos* to Artemis,

ἔνθα ἄχρι ἐμοῦ μονομαχίας ἆθλα ἦν καὶ ἱερᾶσθαι τῇ θεῷ τὸν νικῶντα· ὁ δὲ ἀγὼν ἐλευθέρων μὲν προέκειτο
οὐδενὶ οἰκέταις δὲ ἀποδρᾶσι τοὺς δεσπότας. [2.27.4: ... where down to my time prizes of single combat are
the victor's service to the goddess as priest; the contest is not open to any freeman, but to slaves
who have run away from their masters.]

Pausanias confirms Servius' *monomachia*: there was a combat between challenger
and incumbent, both having come to Aricia as fugitive slaves; the winner became
or remained Diana's priest.

  With one exception (Suetonius) there remain only poetic allusions to the Arician
priesthood. In his *Art of Love* (1.259–260) Ovid mentions the woodland temple
of suburban Diana *partaque per gladios regna nocente manu,* the kingship won
with swords. In the *Fasti,* in a passage on the Arician sanctuary, Ovid alludes to
the kingship that a runaway holds after killing his predecessor:

regna tenent fortes manibus pedibusque fugaces
et perit exemplo postmodo quisque suo.   (3.271–272)

This is a poetic statement of the rule of succession: the fugitive who is strong of
arm and fleet of foot can win the kingship. Valerius Flaccus merely alludes to the
custom in *soli non mitis Aricia regi* (*Arg.* 2.305). When Statius says *profugis cum
regibus aptum / fumat Aricinum Triviae nemus* (*Silv.* 3.1.55–56), he is more
likely, as Lang supposes (1901:209), to be referring to Hippolytos and Orestes,
princes who fled to Aricia, as Greco-Italian legend had it, than to the rule of
succession to the priesthood (we must then take *regibus* as proleptic).

THE SUCCESSION COMBAT

There remains one other notice of the Rex Nemorensis. In his *Life of Caligula*
(35), Suetonius says of that unpleasant emperor: *nullus denique tam abjectae
condicionis tamque extremae sortis fuit cuius non commodis obtrectaret. nemor-
ensi regi quod multos jam annos poteretur sacerdotio validiorem adversarium
subornavit.* Men of humble origin were not beneath Caligula's envious notice.
A King of the Woods who had held the post many years attracted his attention,
and Caligula engaged a stronger man to fight him. This means presumably that
he hired a runaway slave to do the job, since he would have to follow the cult
law; that is, he had to arrange for a slave to escape and reach Diana's grove.
So either the slave was his own, or he instructed an owner (probably paying him)
to connive at the slave's escape. Where would Caligula look to find a slave who
would be *validior adversarius*? Obviously among gladiators, most of whom were
slaves: Caligula found his king-elect in a *ludus*. Here we have evidence of great
significance for an interpretation of the "ghastly priest."

  Suetonius' context is revealing: the Rex Nemorensis is one of three men of low
condition who attracted Caligula's invidious notice. Another was Aesius Proculus,

---

[a] Servius, it is true, has *dabatur autem fugitivis potestas ut siquis exinde ramum potuisset
auferre,* etc. This may mean that someone might try to keep a fugitive from the tree; but it may
also refer to the slave's success in escaping to the tree where he can pluck a bough.

called Colosseros, a tall and handsome man. Caligula had him dragged from his seat into the arena and forced him to fight two gladiators; when Colosseros defeated both, Caligula had him bound, humiliated, and finally strangled. On another occasion Caligula objected to the applause given Porius, an *essedarius,* when after a victory this man freed a slave. Both Colosseros and Porius appear to have been freemen (or freedmen); but Porius was a gladiator, and Colosseros, if not himself a gladiator (he was probably *miles;* his father was a *primipilaris*), fought in gladiatorial combats on the last day of his life—very seldom did a citizen fight in the arena. Thus all three examples in *Caligula* 35 are gladiatorial, and the Rex is placed between the other two.

May we suppose that the succession combat at Aricia was a gladiatorial bout, or something very like it? That is, was it a match between gladiators, between slaves who fought with swords? Was it perhaps a scheduled public event at a religious festival? It may be significant that the very first painting of gladiatorial games was placed by C. Terentius Lucanus in Diana's grove (Pliny *NH* 35.33.52: *in nemore Dianae* can mean only the grove near Aricia): this was a goddess who liked gladiatorial combat. If the priest's combat was gladiatorial, it is reasonable to suppose that it took place only on fixed days as a feature of a festival.

One day on which Diana's priest could be challenged was surely the Ides of August (13th), the day of Diana's festival at Aricia and on the Aventine, where the Arician cult had a Roman branch.[7] This day was also the day of a slaves' festival, as Plutarch tells us in his *Roman Questions.* All slave men and women, he says, celebrate a festival on that day and are free of work for the day.[8] He adds that women, both slave and free, wash their heads on this day, and he supposes that the custom spread from slave women to free. Plutarch's allusion to the women's observance, which he attaches to the slaves' festivities on the same day, assures us that it was Diana's festival which the slaves were celebrating on August 13, although he mentions no deity. For Diana's festival of the August Ides was very much a women's festival. According to Ovid,

> saepe potens voti, frontem redimita coronis,
> femina lucentes portat ab urbe faces.[9]

Since the succession combat was fought between slaves, and the victor became Diana's priest, it was very likely an event of the slaves' festival celebrated in Diana's honor. Moreover it is consistent with the known programs of ancient festivals to conclude that the succession combat was a feature of Diana's festival on the Ides, and probably the principal event of the day. There was also a dog

[7] *CIL* 6.2298; Varro, *Lingua Latina* 5.43; Festus, p. 467 Lindsay. These citations have reference to Diana's cult on the Aventine; for the festival at Aricia see Stat. *Silv.* 3.1.55–60. The Arician Diana's cult on the Aventine did not have a Rex Nemorensis.

[8] *QR* 100 = *Mor.* 287EF: Διὰ τί ταῖς Αὐγούσταις εἰδοῖς Σεξτιλίαις δὲ πρότερον λεγομέναις ἑορτάζουσιν αἵ τε δοῦλαι καὶ οἱ δοῦλοι πάντες . . . ; Ἡ διὰ τὸ Σερούιον τὸν βασιλέα κατὰ ταύτην τὴν ἡμέραν ἐξ αἰχμαλώτου γενέσθαι θεραπαινίδος ἄδειαν ἔργων ἔχουσιν οἱ θεράποντες, . . . Cf. Festus, pp. 460, 467 Lindsay.

[9] Ovid *Fasti* 3. 269–270; see also *Ars Am.* 1. 259–260. Statius alludes to the women's torches in *et face multa / conscius Hippolyti splendet lacus* (*Silv.* 3.156–57). Festus (p. 67 Lindsay) says that pregnant women made sacrifice to Egeria at Aricia. On the cult and sanctuary of Diana at Aricia, see Lucia Morpurgo 1903 and A. E. Gordon 1934. For Diana in the Latin cities, see F. Altheim 1903: 93–135; K. Latte, *Römische Religionsgeschichte* (Munich: Beck, 1960), pp. 169–173.

race—at least, Diana herself crowned victorious dogs on that day. Hunting spears were cleaned but not used, since wild beasts were allowed to roam freely (just as the slaves were):

> ... ipsa coronat
> emeritos Diana canes et spicula terget
> et tutas sinit ire feras, omnisque pudicis
> Itala terra focis Hecateidas excolit idus.
>
> (Statius, *Silv.* 3.1.57–60)

The succession combat was arranged beforehand, as we may conclude from Suetonius' notice; for his point is not that it was unusual to provide an opponent for the Rex Nemorensis, but that Caligula, the emperor, gave so much invidious attention to such picayunish matters as the affairs of gladiators and the like— it was beneath an emperor's *dignitas*—and that he took the trouble to provide a stronger opponent who could defeat the incumbent priest. It appears, therefore, that ordinarily an opponent was provided (possibly more than one), but that no special effort was made to find a victor: men wanted a fair fight, and if the incumbent won, they accepted the outcome. Probably each combatant had his backers; it may well be that Caligula had lost his wager, placed on the challenger, several years running, and now made sure of winning.

The few notices of the Rex Nemorensis bear out my interpretation. Pausanias uses the technical vocabulary of the games: the priesthood was the prize (*athla*) which went to the victor (*ton nikônta*) in a single combat (*monomachia*), and the contest (*agôn*) was not open to freemen, but was set (*proekeito* as passive of *protithenai,* the technical term for setting a contest or prize) for fugitive slaves only. Ovid's *partaque per gladios regna nocente manu* (*Art of Love* 1.260) points to a gladiatorial combat of which *regna* are the prize, rather than to random en-counters that the priest might have to face at any moment. And Ovid's *regna tenent fortes manibus pedibusque fugaces* (*Fasti* 3.271) indicates a preliminary race: the challenger had to be not only strong of arm but fleet of foot. That is, the men who had charge of this contest designated a likely slave-gladiator as challenger. On the proper day, the Ides of August (and possibly on other holy days), he was sent to the neighborhood of Diana's grove. Perhaps he was instructed to run for the grove from a designated point; men gave chase, and if he reached the grove ahead of them, he had entered asylum and won the race (did the vic-torious dogs and hunting spears have anything to do with this race?) Thus he was technically a runaway slave—although he was free of work on the August Ides, he was not free of servitude. Once within the grove he could perhaps conceal himself and plan his time and movements with respect to combat as he wished; for Strabo says that the priest was on the watch looking in all directions (*periskopôn*) for onsets (*epitheseis*); or was the priest's object to prevent the fugitive from entering the grove if he could—an extra hazard to the racer—not knowing, however, from what direction the fugitive would come?

We can only guess at details, supporting our conjectures by citing the customs of other cults. But we do not have to rely on Ovid's *pedibusque fugaces* (interpreted usually as simply an allusion to the fugitive slave) for evidence of a foot race as preliminary to the combat. From Festus (p. 460 Lindsay), who probably took the information from Varro, we learn that the slave who outran his pursuers was called *cervus;* and Festus says this precisely with respect to Diana's festival: *Servorum dies festus vulgo existimatur Idus Aug., quod eo die Ser. Tullius, natus servus, aedem Dianae dedicaverit in Aventino, cuius tutelae sint cervi; a quo celeritate fugitivos vocent cervos.* August 13 is the slaves' festival day because that is the day on which King Servius Tullius dedicated Diana's temple on the Aventine (to represent the goddess' Arician cult in Rome); Diana protects deer, whence fugitive slaves are called deer for their fleetness of foot. These *cervi* must be those who ran fast on Diana's festival day, whence Diana protected and honored the victorious runners, just as she honored the dogs who ran fast on that same day.[10]

TREE AND BOUGH

When the *cervus* won his race and reached the grove, he had to break a bough from a sacred tree before challenging the priest. Or so Servius the commentator tells us, although he says nothing about how or when the fugitive broke the bough. Did the priest guard the tree and try to keep the would-be challenger off? Was it a wide-spreading tree with low-hanging branches, so that the runaway had a good chance of eluding the priest by reaching the opposite side of the tree and leaping up to pluck a bough? Or did he have the right to a bough if he just reached the tree? We know nothing about it.

Or did he have to pluck a bough at all? Only Servius mentions it; he lived around A.D. 390–400 and spoke of the custom in a past tense: *fuit arbor quaedam, infringi ramum non licebat, dabatur autem fugitivis potestas, fugitivus illic erat sacerdos.* Cult and priesthood and rite had passed away before his time. Furthermore Servius' only authority was *publica opinio.* This does not mean the general public opinion of antiquity or Italian tradition, as Frazer took it, but rather "a common notion," as Conway says (1928:42). In its entirety and essence this *opinio* was the story of Orestes' coming to Aricia with the Tauric Diana's image and barbarous rite, later transmuted into the succession combat. At that point Servius mentions the tree and bough. Need we believe in bough or tree? They rest on very slender evidence. Still, where did Servius get his special tree, if there never had been one? Mistakes, confusions are always possible, and both *publica opinio* and Servius are by no means innocent of them; but we should not lightly assume error. The answer may lie in the inviolability of the whole sacred grove; for surely the mutilation of sacred trees was forbidden to everyone—only a priest might cut a bough under the severest restrictions and only for a sacred purpose. Cult laws in both Italy and Greece forbade the cutting of trees and the taking of wood from sacred groves, and assessed severe penalties for violations, e.g., fifty lashes for a slave, a fine of fifty drachmas for a freeman.[11] We even hear of the

---

[10] Perhaps relevant is Plut. *QG* 39 = *Mor.* 300CD: the intruder in the Lykaion near Lykosura in Arcadia was called *elaphos.* The first man so called was Kantharion, an Arcadian who had deserted to the Eleans in wartime and had crossed the Lykaion with plunder; when the war ended he fled to Sparta; an oracle then ordered the Spartans to surrender the deer. Here a fugitive and sanctuary violator is called "deer." Altheim (1930:143–156) perceives a relation between the Arician combat and gladiatorial games (and also with other kinds of ritual contests), but in his efforts to prove a Greek origin of Diana tries to find antecedents in Greek cults of Artemis.

[11] See *IG*² 1362 = Michel 686, inscription (about 300 B.C.) of a regulation concerning the *temenos* of Apollo Erithaseos at Athens, forbidding the cutting of trees or the taking of wood, twigs, and even fallen leaves from the *temenos:* a slave who violates the decree will receive fifty

death penalty, although it is not attested in inscriptions: Aelian (*VH* 5.17) tells us that the Athenians killed anyone who cut down a holm oak in a *hêrôon*. Festus (p. 57 Lindsay) speaks of *Capitalis lucus, ubi siquid violatum est caput violatoris expiatur.* Diana's grove at Nemi was surely *capitalis lucus.*

Let us suppose that the main task of Diana's priest was to guard the sacred grove from possible violators, a suggestion that others have made.[12] Then on the Ides of August, the slaves' holiday, a runaway slave, according to custom, broke a bough from a tree in the grove, thus violating the taboo; and it was the priest's duty to attack him for doing so. Thus the breaking of a bough was a challenge to combat with the priest, and the priest's duty of punishing or apprehending violators was the pretext for and justification of the festival combat. This interpretation of the bough is consistent with my interpretation of the succession combat as the main feature of Diana's festival.[13] Everything, as we gather from Suetonius' testimony, was arranged beforehand: a gladiator was chosen, who escaped to Diana's grove on the Ides, broke a bough, and thus had combat with the priest, who had been expecting him. By Servius' time, when Diana's cult and the succession combat were no more, "a tree in the grove" from which the fugitive plucked a bough had become (in the tradition) a particular tree.[14]

Strabo's words are consistent with my agonistic interpretation of the Arician custom with or without the bough-breaking. The priest, he says, bearing a sword in hand or scabbard (Strabo simply says *xiphêrês*), kept looking about in expectation of onsets (attacks), ready to ward them off; immediately thereafter, Strabo mentions the grove: ξιφήρης οὖν ἐστιν ἀεὶ περισκοπῶν τὰς ἐπιθέσεις, ἕτοιμος ἀμύνεσθαι. τὸ δ' ἱερὸν ἐν ἄλσει, . . . We may interpret these words in two ways: (1) the King of the Woods was always armed with a sword, but was on the lookout for attacks from challengers only on the festival days for which a combat was planned— although Strabo does not qualify his statement, probably because he knew little

---

lashes; a freeman offender will be fined fifty drachmas. See also *IG* 5.1390 = Michel 694, lines 78–80 (91 B.C.), a law regulating the cult and mysteries of the goddesses at Andania: again a slave violator gets a beating and a freeman is fined. For Italy see *CIL* 11.4766 = Dessau 4911 on a sacred grove at Spoleto; an exception is made only for the wood needed for the regular sacrifices. On the sanctity of groves see Frazer 1911*a*: II, 121–123; Morpurgo 1903:364–365.

[12] Lang (1901:220) supposes that the Rex was *garde champêtre* to a single tree (since he accepts Servius' tree). Gordon (1934:18–19) suggests that the Rex policed the beggars who infested the *clivus Aricinus;* see Morpurgo 1903:366.

[13] After writing this section, I came upon Morpurgo 1903:364–366, who came to a similar conclusion about the breaking of a bough: the fugitive purposely violated the grove in order to challenge the priest, and if he was not killed at once in combat with the priest he was killed later by his successor; still later the violation became "un atto rituale d'importanza secondaria, di cui non si comprendeva il significato, . . . " For Morpurgo, as for Frazer and others, the bough had to be broken from a particular tree, not from any tree in the grove. She also thought that perhaps Servius "ci riferisce non un atto che realmente si compiva, ma che una tradizione locale diceva si dovesse compiere."

[14] It is impossible to suppose that one and the same tree remained for centuries the sacred tree from which the fugitive had to take either a bough or mistletoe. The tree would soon be depleted of mistletoe, especially if candidates for the priesthood were as numerous as Frazer supposed (unless the ancient Italians knew how to graft mistletoe); as Lang puts it, "if the bough was mistletoe, the sacred tree would need to be changed every time (of which we hear nothing), for it is not a case of *Uno avulso non deficit alter* with mistletoe" (1901:221). Or the tree would in time become mutilated and shorn, if each fugitive cut a bough from it, since cut boughs do not replace themselves (not very soon anyway). Of course, much depends on the number of fugitives who came and the intervals. Moreover trees grow old and die. Frazer has a single tree that stood for at least 1500 years, to which fugitives were constantly coming, and which kept reproducing the mistletoe that they hacked away.

about the Arician cult;[15] (2) the King of the Woods wore the sword as the badge and weapon of his office, in which his chief duty was to police the grove and protect it from wood-gatherers or from unlawful trespassers. In the latter interpretation the expected *epitheseis* are unlawful invasions of the grove.[16] Perhaps Strabo has merged both meanings into one sentence; his "ever sword-bearing" points to the priest's constant police duties and the rest of his sentence to the priest's behavior on the combat day.

The rule of succession, therefore, as Strabo, Pausanias, and Servius state it, was the rationale of a festival event, a gladiatorial combat between incumbent priest and a challenger. It was a deadly event, as were all gladiatorial combats; but cruel and bloody rites and cult practices were far from unknown in Italy and Greece. This interpretation of the Arician custom makes much more sense than Frazer's and is much more consistent with ancient religious practices. Frazer assumed that every King of the Woods was killed in combat; he never allowed for death from other causes (as from pneumonia from staying out late at night in cold rain or snow to guard the tree). Suppose that the Rex died of a heart attack—what happened then? Probably two men were chosen to fight for the crown.

DIANA VESTA

We must keep in mind that we know very little about Diana's priest. The sources are rather surprisingly few in comparison with the fairly large amount of evidence for the cult itself and for the myth and worship of Virbius and Egeria.[17] As Morpurgo (1903:353) and Gordon (1934:19) point out, the Rex is nowhere mentioned in the inscriptions of Nemi or Aricia. He was probably no more a real priest than he was a real king. He was called *sacerdos* as Diana's servant; his title *Rex* proclaimed him the most recent victor in the gladiatorial contest of Diana's cult; he was the champion (see Lang 1901:222). The added *Nemorensis* indicated his duty: he was warden of the grove. The kingly title, perhaps a popular pleasantry at first, became sanctified by usage and tradition.

True enough, neither inscriptions nor literature mention any other priest or priestess of Diana Nemorensis. Ordinarily a goddess would have a priestess.[18]

---

[15] The ἀεί modifies ξιφήρης; to take it with περισκοπῶν would give it undue emphasis as first word in the participial phrase. Again it may be taken as "on each occasion," equivalent to ἑκάστοτε, which may be its primary signification. That is, on every festival day the priest carried a sword, on guard for attacks.

[16] The middle voice of ἀμύνεσθαι may be an objection to this interpretation; but in protecting the grove against destructive intruders the King was also protecting his office, and in any instance of combat with a trespasser necessarily defending himself. Furthermore Strabo, informed only by report, may not have understood the custom.

[17] As Lang says (1901:209, 218), the Hippolytos and Orestes legends are obviously late importations into the cult tradition; and like so many cult myths, they do not really fit the rituals and cult institutions, since neither prince was a fugitive slave, and Hippolytos did not kill a predecessor; as for Orestes, nothing is said about his cutting a bough, and his visit to Aricia is never related to his killing of Aigisthos. There is obviously no relation between the Arician succession combat and the legendary Tauric sacrifice, as Servius and others believed: Serv. *Aen.* 2.116, 6.136; Solin. 2.11; Val. Flacc. *Arg.* 2.300–305; Strabo 5.3.12, p. 239. The two rites have in common only the general quality of barbarity; there is little similarity between the combat to death and the sacrifice of every foreigner who comes to the land.

[18] Latte, *op. cit.*, p. 171: . . . bleibt ein männlicher Priester für eine Frauengottheit sehr auffällig."

That a priestess presided over the Arician Diana's cult is the more likely in that this Diana was identified with Vesta, as an inscription of Nemi shows.[19] Frazer supposed a hearth burning with an undying fire in Diana Vesta's temple. Such a hearth is unattested; but fire played a prominent part in the Arician Diana's worship (Ovid, *Fasti* 3.270: Statius, *Silv.* 3.1.56–57); and Statius completes his description of Diana's festival day with *omnisque pudicis / Itala terra focis Hecateidas excolit idus* ("and the whole land celebrates Hecate's [i.e., Artemis'] Ides at chaste hearths"). If household hearths blazed on Diana's Ides, it was probably because of the hearth's significance in her worship: she was the hearth-goddess, called Diana in the Alban Hills. If so, a virgin priestess served her, assisted by Vestals who kept the hearth fire burning always. The rule of chastity in her cult, her patronage of women in pregnancy and childbirth, and the worship of her in a grove where she protected game and trees, and where she was patroness of hunters, caused Greeks and Italians to identify her with Artemis rather than with Hestia, especially since she was not ordinarily called Vesta at Aricia.[20] The priestess and virgin attendants may be reflected in the nymphs who in Ovid's story of Egeria (*Metam.* 15.487–492), tried to console Egeria when she disturbed Diana's Arician rites with her laments for the dead Numa. A terra-cotta bust found at Nemi has been identified as as Vestal Virgin; and if Fundilia Rufa, whose portrait bust on a marble stele was found at Nemi, has been correctly identified as Diana's priestess, inasmuch as she has the hairdress of Diana as seen on gold and silver coins of Augustus' reign, then we have strong evidence that a priestess and Vestals were Diana's ministrants and that the Rex had little or nothing to do with her rites.[21]

VIRBIUS AND EGERIA

Since this Diana of Aricia was the Latin Vesta, we can understand why she was the chief goddess of the Latin League. Hers was an ancient Italian cult, a cult of the League's hearth-goddess and of two subordinate and attendant figures, Virbius and Egeria. The identification of Diana with Artemis soon obscured the aboriginal and indigenous character of this cult. With Artemis came the myths of Hippolytos and Orestes, the consequent identification of Virbius with Hippolytos, and the enrollment of Egeria in Artemis' band of attendant nymphs. This pair, Virbius and Egeria, hover between deity and humanity in the sources (nothing earlier than the empire): he is the hero Hippolytos who became a god, even identified with Sol (Serv. Auct. *Aen.* 7.776), in Diana's grove—but he is also *bis vir* as Diana's companion at Nemi (Serv. *Aen.* 7.761); she is nymph and goddess (Ovid *Fasti* 3.275), and also wife of King Numa. They are each a type of supernatural being, frequent in Italy and Greece, that may be called hero, demigod, godling, daimōn,

---

[19] *CIL* 14.2213: Dianae nemoresi Vestae sacrum dict. imp. Nerva Traiano Aug. Germanico.

[20] I can therefore agree with A. E. Gordon that Diana is a native Italian goddess: see 1934: 8–13 and "On the Origin of Diana," *TAPhA* LXIII (1932), 177–192. Diana, I would say, is particularly a Latin goddess, the Vesta of the Alban Hills and Algidus. See A. Alföldi, "Diana Nemorensis," *AJA* 64 (1960), pp. 137–144 and plates 31–34.

[21] G. H. Wallis, *Illustrated Catalogue of Classical Antiquities from the Site of the Temple of Diana, Nemi, Italy* (Nottingham, 1893), p. 30, no. 600; p. 52, no. 827; Morpurgo 1903: 350. For coins see H. Mattingly, *Catalogue of Coins of the Roman Empire in the British Museum*, I, p. 21, nos. 104–106 (pl. 4.2–3 rev.); p. 83, no. 488 (pl. 12.9 rev.).

or spirit—the ancients appear to have been as uncertain as we. We should notice how many native and characteristically Italian deities were, like Virbius, identified with figures of legend: Mater Matuta with Ino, Carmentis with Evander's mother, Bona Dea with Fauna, Anna Perenna with Dido's sister Anna, Quirinus with Romulus. None of these legendary figures was a real person, I am sure (I make haste to disclaim Euhemerism); but the ancient Italians believed that all these deities had lived as mortal men on earth. So persistent was the belief, so frequent the phenomenon, throughout the Mediterranean world—where the cult of saints carries on the same tradition—that we may reasonably suppose these figures to have begun as heroes, i.e., as powerful ghosts. A hero or saint becomes a local power, i.e., a deity, good for the crops or healing or navigation, identified with trees and rocks and springs, as Egeria with a spring at Nemi (Ovid *Fasti* 3.275, *Metam.* 15.550–551). Now the cult of heroes is simply the cult of the dead, a public cult of powerful dead as distinguished from the ordinary private worship of dead members of the family or from the public worship of the Manes, the dead in general. It may be that no living man ever bore the hero's name; the point is that his worshipers believed that he had once lived as a mortal man. Once men have heroes and saints and deities, they create new forms on the old models (that is, not every god starts out as a hero; and some gods, in fact, sink to hero status).

There once lived in Latium women named Egeria: every woman of the Egerian gens bore that name. It was a man of that gens who dedicated Diana's grove at Aricia. Cato the Censor called him Egerius Baebius (or Laevius) of Tusculum, *dictator Latinus;* according to Festus, his name was Manius Egerius, from whom were descended many illustrious men.[22] Manius Egerius Baebius (Laevius) may be a purely legendary figure, but if so the *Tusculanus* which Cato attached to his name is hard to explain; why from Tusculum rather than from Aricia?[23] And if he is only a legendary figure, why does the tradition make him just dedicator of the grove, and not of the whole sanctuary and cult?

If *Egeria* is a gentile name, may not *Virbius* be also, the legendary eponym of a Latin gens? There is some indication of this in *Aeneid* 7.761–764:

> Ibat et Hippolyti proles pulcherrima bello,
> Virbius, insignem quem mater Aricia misit,
> eductum Egeriae lucis umentia circum
> litora, pinguis ubi et placabilis ara Dianae.

Among the Latin chiefs gathered for war upon the Trojans was Virbius, son of Hippolytos-Virbius (and Aricia?). Most of these chiefs—especially those who play no significant part in the epic—are eponyms: Aventinus, Coras, Messapus, Clausus,

---

[22] Cato Cens. *ap.* Prisc. *Inst.* 4.21 (I 129 Hertz); Festus, p. 128 Lindsay. Cato supplies the *cognomen*, Festus the *praenomen*.

[23] See Morpurgo 1903: 342–343 on the historicity of Egerius Laevius (Baebius). The name *Egerius* appears also as *agnomen* of Tarquinius Arruns, whom his uncle, Tarquinius Priscus, made ruler of Collatia. Since he lacked an inheritance, he was called *Egerius,* i.e., Needy. See Dion. Hal. *Ant. Rom.* 3.50.3, Livy 1.34.2–3. Collatia is about twelve miles from Tusculum. According to Dion. Hal. the Romans gave the name *Egerius* to poor men and beggars, although nothing in extant Latin texts substantiates his statement; but it recalls the information that beggars (perhaps called *Manii,* supposedly after the Tusculan Egerius' *praenomen*) infested the *clivus Virbi* at Aricia; see Pers. 6.55–60; Juv. 4.116–118; Festus, p. 128 Lindsay. But we know too little about either Tusculan or Etruscan Egerius to establish a relation between them. See Altheim 1930:130.

Halaesus, Ufens, Umbro. They are mostly eponyms of cities and lands. But one gentile eponym appears among them, *Clausus:*

> Claudia nunc a quo diffunditur et tribus et gens
> per Latium, postquam in partem data Roma Sabinis.
> *(Aen.* 7.708–709)

One may object that if there was a Virbian gens, its eponymous ancestor ought not to bear the gentile name itself, an adjectival form—we should not have a Virbius as ancestor of every Virbius—but a name like *Virbus,* from which the gentilic designation would be supposedly derived. The Claudian gens, supposedly deriving its name from Clausus, illustrates the usual relation of eponym to gentilic: the latter is an adjectival form derived from the former (actually or traditionally: often the eponymous ancestor is a later construction made from the gentilic adjective). There are, however, other than gentilic names which end in *ius,* e.g., Mezentius, Appius, Manius. And since in the *Aeneid* Virbius is father of Virbius, we perceive that in this instance the eponym is identical in name with the gens sup-supposedly descended from him. Probably the hero-god Virbius was in origin a projection of the Virbian gens.

The Latin chief was son of Virbius and Aricia (Aricia was either mother or motherland). This was an Arician gens. Virbius and an Egeria as deities of the grove represented gentes who founded and maintained the sanctuary (it was Virbius-Hippolytos who founded Artemis' *temenos,* according to Pausanias 2.27.4). We need not suppose an actual Virbius and an actual Egeria who once lived and died and who after death received heroic honors and worship in Diana-Vesta's grove. The fact is that their worshippers took them to be historical. Each represents a whole gens including all its dead.[24] Yet neither apparently had a tomb: Virbius lurked in the grove, and the dead Egeria was transformed into a spring: grove and spring were in effect the tombs.[25] The identification of Virbius with Hippolytos affected his cult: he became Artemis' chaste companion who rose from death to presumably immortal life as a god. But Virgil has the original Italian Virbius, who had a wife and son.[26] It may be that in the earliest days of the Arician cult a tomb of Virbius could be seen in the grove.

---

[24] We may wonder why the Egerian gens was represented by a woman. She could not be reputed ancestress of the *gens Egeria* as Virbius could be ancestor of the *gens Virbia.* Nor was she represented as mate of Virbius (except in Sil. Ital. 4.380, probably a misinterpretation of Virg. *Aen.* 7.761–763), reflecting marriage alliances of the two gentes: in legend she was wife of King Numa. We may notice that her name is the adjectival form which modifies *gens;* she has the name of the gens itself as distinct from any member of it. So she was perhaps the spirit of the gens, a kind of mother spirit (but not ancestress), in whom the gens placed its hopes of abundant progeny. Notice Festus, p. 67 Lindsay: *Egeriae nymphae sacrificabant praegnantes quod eam putabant facile conceptum alvo egerere.* From gentile spirit she became protectress of all women. On Egeria as *Gentilgottheit* see Altheim 1930: 94. Perhaps the priestess of Diana in earlier days was always an Egeria, and from this custom the goddess Egeria was projected; possibly because this gens had died out we find that a Fundilia Rufa was priestess in Trajan's reign.

[25] Ovid's *Metam.* alone offers several tales of springs (e.g., Byblis, Arethusa) and of trees (e.g., Philemon and Baucis, Dryope) into which human beings had been transformed; this was the death of the mortal person (whose historical existence was generally unquestioned), who then had no other tomb. The identification of trees and springs with dead persons is common; see Frazer 1911a: II, 29–33 for trees. In *To a God Unknown* John Steinbeck has imaginatively grasped the primitive feelings and conceptions through which a dead father becomes a tree spirit; see Fontenrose, *John Steinbeck: An Introduction and Interpretation* (New York: Barnes & Noble, 1963), pp. 13, 16–18.

[26] Virgil's *quem mater Aricia misit* may mean only that the town of Aricia, the younger Virbius'

MUNERA

If the cults of Virbius and Egeria were originally cults of heroized ancestors, a form of the worship of the dead, there should be nothing surprising about the presence of gladiatorial combat among cult observances. The institution of funeral games and of games in commemoration of the dead was ancient in Greece and Italy. It may be that games and contests in honor of the dead preceded agonistic festivals of gods: the Iliad has accounts of funeral games and no others, whereas the first quinquennial agonistic festival, the Olympian, was not founded until 776 B.C.[27] But whatever the origin of *ludi* and *munera*, wherever they first appeared as features of worship, they were celebrated in the worship of the dead from early times until the end of Greco-Roman paganism. And whatever may be true of other sorts of games in Italy, the earliest gladiatorial combats appear to have been primarily funerary at first. They were *munera*, services to the dead; in the late republic and empire *munera* commonly meant gladiatorial exhibitions, then held on all sorts of occasions.[28]

Varro (*ap.* Serv. Auct. *Aen.* 3.67) placed the origin of gladiatorial combats at the funeral of Junius Brutus in 509 B.C. It had been the custom, he said, to make animal and human sacrifices at funerals. When the gentes sent very many captives to be slaughtered in Brutus' honor, his grandson hit upon the idea of matching them in pairs for combat, *et quod muneri missi erant inde munus appellatum:* since the captives had been sent for a "service," the combat was therefore called "service." We can put little trust in this evidence. It is much more certain that the first gladiatorial combats held in Rome took place in 264 B.C. (consulship of Appius Claudius and Quintus Fulvius) at the funeral of Brutus Pera (perhaps confusion of names led to the tradition that Junius Brutus' funeral was the occasion); the dead man's sons held them in the Forum Boarium: *nam gladiatorum munus primum Romae datum est in foro boario App. Claudio Q. Fulvio consulibus. dederunt Marcus et Decimus filii Bruti Perae funebri memoria patris cineres honorando* (Val. Max. 2.4.7). We may now recall that Diana's Arician grove received the first painting of gladiatorial games, according to the elder Pliny (p. 40 above). It is now clear that the offering of C. Terentius Lucanus had a special relevance to Diana's cult: her grove was the scene of gladiatorial combat. This combat was a festival event in the worship of ancestral deities, Virbius and Egeria, associated with Diana-Vesta, the common hearth of the united Latin gentes. It may have begun at funeral games in honor of some great Latin, possibly a Virbius or

---

motherland, sent him off to war. Or *mater Aricia* could be Diana (Arician mother), but would Virgil suppose a mating of Hippolytos-Virbius and Artemis-Diana? Still the elder Virbius, having become a father, must have had a mate, and whoever she was, she was Arician. On Virbius' mate see G. Radke, *RE* 9A.179, and for speculations on the derivation of *Virbius*, none very convincing, *ibid.* 180–182. We should notice that the image of Virbius was taboo (Serv. Auct. *Aen.* 7.776: *cuius simulacrum non est fas attingere*) and that horses were not allowed in the Arician sanctuary and grove, allegedly because horses had killed Hippolytos (Vir. *Aen.* 7.778–780; Ovid *Fasti* 3.265–266). One may speculate about possible connections between forbidden *equi* and welcome *cervi* or victorious *canes,* and between the image which nobody could touch and the tree from which nobody could pluck a bough except fugitive slaves.

[27] See André Piganiol, *Recherches sur les jeux romains* (Strasbourg, Paris: Istra, 1923), pp. 20, 69, 135, 146; F. Altheim, *A History of Roman Religion* (London: Methuen, 1938), p. 289.

[28] Piganiol, *op. cit.*, pt. 2, ch. v; Altheim, *Hist. Rom. Rel.*, pp. 48, 286.

Egerius, when two violators of the grove, both fugitive slaves, were matched against each other. The Latins set the rules: the victor could not leave the grove which he had desecrated; he should stay as keeper until the next occasion or anniversary, when he would have to face a competitor, another fugitive. Although this reconstruction of the origin of the combat is highly conjectural, it seems to me much more probable than Frazer's, namely, that the combat at Nemi was a degraded survival of a succession combat fought for a real divine kingship.

Since Diana's festival day, the August Ides, was a day of freedom for slaves, and since the keeper of the grove had to be a slave, Andrew Lang's suggestion that her grove was once an asylum for fugitives seems probable.[29] Lang is less convincing in his whole hypothesis, which he grants to be conjectural, though, unlike Frazer's theory, it does not require the introduction of a single extraneous factor. Lang supposes that since "an unlimited asylum of fugitive slaves was an inconvenient neighbour to Aricia," the right of asylum "was at last limited to one fugitive slave at a time," who had to guard a single tree (Lang accepts the single tree); any fugitive slave who wanted asylum there had to remove the current holder of the right, and he broke a bough from the tree as a challenge to combat. Rather, asylum for fugitives was probably unlimited at all times (as was the rule in other asyla). A fugitive slave could not lawfully be killed or injured in the grove or dragged away from it. But was anyone obliged to feed him or give him shelter from bad weather? Much depended upon the cult officials, nearness of friends who could bring food, and other circumstances. If a fugitive, subject to seizure as soon as he crossed the asylum boundary, where pursuers awaited him, could not get food, hunger would drive him to kill a deer or rabbit in the grove, and to cut boughs for firewood. Once he had violated the grove, he could be seized. And so on one occasion, I have supposed, two such violators were set to fight each other with swords.

In making or assessing any conjecture about the King of the Woods we must constantly keep in mind how unique this institution was in Italy and in the whole Mediterranean world, how unparalleled anywhere—it is hard to find anything remotely like it. Frazer's African and Indian parallels are dubious and at best dissimilar. The nearest parallel is the title bout in prize fighting.

Nothing better illustrates Frazer's way of dealing with evidence and of drawing conclusions from it than his chapter on the King of the Woods, the initial chapter of *The Golden Bough*. He was unreliable in interpretation and induction: he saw less than the evidence allowed, since he failed to interpret words and phrases correctly; and he saw a good deal more than the evidence allowed, since he filled the gaps with imaginary pictures and ill-considered analogies. Whether kings were ever ritually slain or not, the humble office of King of the Woods surely had nothing to do with the practice.

---

[29] Lang 1901: 218–223. On the Arician Diana as protectress of slaves, see Altheim 1930: 143–145.

IV

DEFINITION

THE MYTH-RITUAL RELATION

OVER TWENTY YEARS AGO Clyde Kluckhohn (1942) talked a good deal of sense in a long paper on myths and rituals. He showed that a ritual may be uniform over a large territory, whereas the mythological *aitia* of this ritual may be diverse, different in every community. He found all sorts of relations between myths and rituals among primitive peoples: a ritual drama may clearly enact the events of a myth, or a myth may account for nearly every act in a rite, each ritual act in order; other myths, however, account for rites in a less systematic way; still others tell only how the rites were introduced. Moreover once ritual and myth become associated, one affects the other. The myth suggests additions to the rite (thus helping to build a ritual drama), and the rite suggests additions to or interpolations in the myth. Kluckhohn, who studied primitive societies at first hand, affirms what Raglan and Hyman deny—that myths, as well as rituals, may have their origins in dreams and visions.[1]

Kluckhohn rightly called for "a detailed analysis of actual associations" of myth and ritual. For surely, if the ritualists are right, we should be able to see a one-to-one correspondence, or something like it, between a ritual program and the myth expressly associated with it, whenever we know both the myth text and the ritual sequence (whether from text or direct observation). This sort of study the ritualists have not made in a systematic way. There is no place where Frazer or Harrison or Raglan or Hyman has made a detailed analytic comparison. Theodor Gaster makes a show of doing so in *Thespis* (1950:6–72), but in reality he remains on an abstract level, content to show that rituals and myths alike move through a sequence of mortification, purgation, invigoration, and jubilation. In any story, after all, the hero must fall before he can rise. In *Python* (chapter xv) I attempted an analytic comparison of the program of the Babylonian New Year festival with the *Enuma elish* text, which was read twice during the festival; of the ritual statements of the Egyptian Ramesseum Dramatic Papyrus with the myth statements in it; and of the rites of the Delphic Septerion with the Apollo-Python myth (these are instances in which we are well informed on both myth and rites). I found almost no correspondence at all; the connection was mainly in the statement that the rituals commemorated the mythical events. I was therefore convinced that whatever the origin of these myths, it was not in these rituals. For, it seemed to me, if a myth is a ritual text, then the mythical events should be recognizable in the ritual acts.

We do, of course, find some fairly exact correspondence of myth and ritual, both in the Old World and the New. Wherever this happens the ritual is in fact a ritual drama, and in every instance we may suppose that it was purposely designed to enact the myth. Surely ancient Greek tragedy, the mystery and miracle plays, and the Japanese Nō plays were constructed on previously formed myths. We

---

[1] For other critiques of the ritual theory see Bascom 1957; Greenway 1964: 283–286.

cannot say that these plots either grew up with or grew out of the acts performed. This is also true, I believe, of ritual drama in primitive societies. And if it is true, scholars can reconstruct the missing parts of ritual-drama texts from known myths without being forced to conclude that the myth and ritual grew up together, or that the myth is derived from the ritual. The ritual interpretation, if correct, should enable one to deduce ritual from myth and myth from ritual. Some ritualists in fact maintain that just this sort of thing has been done, for example, in the study of American Indian myths and rituals. However, I can find no instance in which anything has been done other than the kind of reconstruction, the completion of one text or program from the other, already mentioned. Moreover one generally finds dramatic rituals rather than ritual dramas among American Indians: no story is enacted and no story can convincingly be deduced from the ritual texts.

For example, the Iroquois songs or chants which accompany the rites of the Condolence Council do not contain any mythical narrative, and the ritual acts do not enact a story; they are rites performed at the installation of a new chief in the League senate after the death of a chief. The songs allude to the founding of the League, and the first part of the rites is a roll call of the founders. Even if one doubts the historicity of Hiawatha, Deganawideh, and the rest, they are mentioned only as founders of the League and the rites; mythical and legendary themes are completely absent. The ritual purpose is the reuniting, the restrengthening of Iroquois society.[2]

If we turn to the Raingod ceremony of the Tewa at San Juan pueblo in New Mexico, we again find a sequence of ritual acts accompanied by songs and speeches, but no myth. Although Vera Laski calls this a drama, "the story of a people and their gods," it does not in fact enact a story. It is dramatic ritual in which the community summons the Raingods. The principal actors are Clowns and Kachinas (representing Raingods); caciques, priestesses, and the whole community take part. The Clowns improvise somewhat, but most speeches and songs are fixed. It is a magical ritual; its intention is to bring the rain; why else should Raingods be summoned?[3]

---

[2] See Horatio Hale, *The Iroquois Book of Rites*, 2d ed., (Univ. Toronto Press, 1963), pp. 116–145 for text, chapters iii–vii for Hale's discussion of the rites, and pp. xxiii–xxv of the Introduction for W. N. Fenton's remarks on the rites. See also W. N. Fenton, *The Roll Call of the Iroquois Chiefs* (Washington: Smithsonian Inst., 1950); *American Indian and White Relations to 1830* (Chapel Hill: Univ. North Carolina Press, 1957), pp. 22–24; *An Outline of Seneca Ceremonies at Coldspring Longhouse*, Yale University Publications in Anthropology, no. 9 (New Haven: Yale Univ. Press, 1936). In a letter, which I quote with his permission, Mr. Fenton kindly informs me that his witnessing of the condolence rites, after working through the ritual texts with Iroquois informants, was invaluable for his understanding and translation of that part of the Iroquois Deganawideh epic which tells about the origin of the Iroquois League; for, he says, the epic "contains toward the end a great deal of built in ritual material"; the Iroquois project into their myths the events and features with which they are familiar, and so, if the myth (or epic) needs a ritual episode, they insert a known ritual. This evidence does not support the ritualists' contentions. On the contrary, the epic ritual material is clearly separate from the main narrative; the epic as a whole is not a ritual text; and the Book of Rites is not part of the epic. Mr. Fenton, furthermore, does not believe that all Iroquois myths have a ritual origin, saying that those which "involve rituals contain a great deal of material that is fed back into the myth from the performance of a ceremony"—exactly as I showed in *Python*, chapter xv.

[3] Vera Laski, *Seeking Life* (Philadelphia: American Folklore Soc., 1958), pp. 34–59 for Raingod Drama text, pp. 60–74 for interpretation. She shows the influence of Frazer and the ritual school: this accounts in part for her interpretation of the Raingod ceremony as drama (pp. 60–63); it is not a tragedy, she grants, but still has a Shakespearean quality: "Like all serious drama, like life itself, it is based on sacrifice," but all that she can show is a maiden's symbolic offering of

The chantways of the nearby Navaho are also dramatic rituals. "The chantways are performed to cure illness," says Katherine Spencer; that is, they too are magical in intent. A myth accompanies each chantway, but the rite does not enact the myth. The myth tells the story of the chantway's origin: a hero, after trials and exploits, went to the sky or otherwise encountered supernatural beings, from whom he learned a chantway; he took this chantway to earth and taught it to his people; then he went back to the supernaturals.[4]

The pattern of the chantway myth is widespread in the American west. Resembling it was the visionary experience of the Paiute Wovoka, who in effect put himself into the place of the mythical hero. A cataleptic trance came upon Wovoka at the time of the eclipse of January 1, 1889, which was total in Mason Valley, Nevada.[5] His soul mounted to heaven, as he told the tale, and talked with God, who entrusted him with a Messianic mission on earth. God gave him power over rain, snow, and sun; appointed him his deputy to rule over the west; instructed him in the Ghost Dance and told him to teach it to his people; and revealed to him moral precepts and prophecies of the future. Very soon, God told him, all the Indians, living and dead, would be reunited upon a renewed earth, and they would lead a happy life, free from death, disease, and hardship; game animals would come back to the land; the white man would somehow disappear from America; Jesus was already on earth in the form of a cloud—or Wovoka seems sometimes to have represented himself as Jesus come back to earth: Porcupine, a Cheyenne, saw stigmata on Wovoka's face and wrist, but could not see his feet. We may call the events of this vision a myth, since they have a narrative sequence which resembles the chantway pattern mentioned above, infused with Christian millennarianism. The narrative is also the *aition* of a ritual and accompanies the ritual, the Ghost Dance, a wild cyclic dance which continues until all dancers have dropped exhausted to the ground. This dance ritual does not in any way enact the visionary events: it has no dramatic or symbolic correlation with the myth.

The findings of field anthropologists—Kluckhohn, Malinowski, Gifford, Fenton, and many others—point in one direction, to a conclusion that myths are generally not ritual texts. Rather they are often recited at public gatherings or in council, on summer nights among some peoples, on winter nights among others.[6]

DEFINITION OF MYTH AND OTHER TERMS

In discussion of myth origins much difficulty arises from the various meanings currently given to the word *myth;* hence profuse semantic tangles. Raglan and Har-

---

her virginity. Laski's comparison of the pueblo rites with the Eleusinian mysteries is unsound (p. 66); for the latter she relied on Frazer, who reported a good deal of fantasy, built up from poor sources. She should look at George E. Mylonas, *Eleusis and the Eleusinian Mysteries* (Princeton Univ. Press, 1961), ch. ix.

[4] See Katherine Spencer, *Mythology and Values* (Philadelphia: American Folklore Soc., 1957), pp. 11–12, 18–30 for definition and pattern, pp. 100–218 for abstracts of myths.

[5] The authoritative account of Wovoka and the Ghost Dance movement is James Mooney, *The Ghost-Dance Religion and the Sioux Outbreak of 1890* (Washington, 1896); see especially pp. 771–791.

[6] Kluckhohn 1942: 64; Malinowski 1926: 50–54; E. W. Gifford, *The Southeastern Yavapai*, University of California Publications in American Archaeology and Ethnology, Vol. 29, No. 3 (Berkeley: University of California Press, 1932), p. 242.

rison have said that myths are the words which accompany rites (so that, as Raglan seriously tells us, the phrase "good-bye [God be with you]" is the myth which accompanies the rite of handshaking at leavetaking). They have no difficulty in demonstrating that a form of words always accompanies rituals. Well and good: if the meaning of the word *myth* could by common agreement be confined to the verbal formulae of rituals, we would be making a tautological definition and nothing else. But then Raglan transfers the statements that may be true about ritual formulae to the traditional narratives which all men have called myths, and he maintains that his definition applies to them also. Suddenly a simple formula of leave-taking becomes the same thing as the tales of Deukalion's flood and of Thor's visit to Jötunheim, simply because we have applied the same term to both. This is the primary semantic error. And when Raglan and Hyman try to bridge the gap between the formulae and the narratives, they get into trouble.

Plainly, as William Bascom has said (1957:114), mythologists and folklorists must agree upon a definition of myth. This is not the Platonic question "What is myth?," implying some ideal entity that is really myth, which our limited mortal vision cannot clearly perceive. It is the question "What phenomena do we designate when we use the term *myth?*" In both scholarly and popular usage *myth* has acquired a variety of meanings; we throw traditional tales, magico-religious beliefs, theology, false beliefs, superstitions, ritual formulae, literary images and symbols, and social ideals into a common pot and call the mixture mythology. The ritualists like Raglan and Hyman deliberately cultivate this state of affairs; they will not have any distinctions: we live in a ritually derived world. Obviously if the tales began as ritual texts, if the gods are projections of ritual acts and emotions, then religion, belief, pantheon, and myth have a single root and are merely different phases of the same thing.

Others than ritualists use the term *mythology* loosely to cover all lore about gods and spirits, whether narrative or not. If one looks into *Asiatic Mythology* (J. Hackin and others) or the recent Larousse *Mythologies,* edited by Pierre Grimal, one will find pantheon, forms of worship, beliefs about gods and afterlife—everything that we mean by religion and theology—subsumed under the term *mythology.* And it is just this kind of usage which leads to the outmoded, but still current definition of mythology as prescientific man's attempt to explain the world about him and its origins. That is, those who thus define myth are thinking of such statements as "God created the world," "Zeus sends the rain," and the like; they are usually not thinking about the tales which we call myths. Their definition will suit creation myths (although it is of no use for interpreting the narrative episodes, or for making clear why beginnings were "explained" in story form); but how well does it suit the myths of Thor's visit to Jötunheim, Orpheus and Eurydike, Artemis and Aktaion, Orion's adventures (concerning which it is patently absurd to say that the whole Orion cycle was devised to explain a certain configuration in the sky; although once Orion was identified with the constellation, his stellar character could wash back into the myth and introduce such an episode as his pursuit of the Pleiades)? The confusion of myths with statements of cosmological belief has created a standard intellectualistic view of myth, which the ritualists have opposed without understanding what is really wrong about it, since they agree with their opponents on the content of mythology and differ only about origins. Of course, rituals, magic, beliefs, myths, are related phenomena in that all are concerned with or directed towards supernatural powers of various sorts; but not to distinguish among them is like lumping all branches of natural science under the term "physics" or "natural philosophy," and never distinguishing physiology from mechanics or chemistry. We lack a satisfactory single term that would cover all supernatural lore; *demonology* might do, but is apt to be misunderstood (perhaps we can move nearer to the Greek and say *daimonology*).

We cannot do much about popular usage, but whatever the relation of myths to other phenomena, I suggest that scholars restrict the term *myth* to those traditional tales which have always been known as myths, and which everyone agrees on calling myths, regardless of whatever other phenomena he may want to include within the term. These are the traditional tales of the deeds of *daimones:* gods, spirits, and all sorts of supernatural or superhuman beings. That is, when we say *myth* we shall mean a *story* of a certain kind: it is traditional (orally transmitted before it is written down, if ever); it has characters of a certain kind (although other kinds, e.g., human beings and animals, may have roles too); and it has a plot (what Aristotle called *mythos*)—that is, it has a beginning, a middle, and an end. This accords well with the classical Greek use of the word *mythos:* in Homeric epic it meant "speech," covering much the same ground as classical *logos;* but in Attic and later Greek, when *logos* came into general use for "speech," *mythos* was restricted to the meaning "story." For the serious student of myth, then, the rule shall be "no story, no myth." He will apply the term *myth* only to traditional tales, or to episodes in them, and the adjective *mythical* only to the events and distinctive contents of such tales. This means that he will not refer to a god as mythical, since this implies that the god is a character in a tale and nothing else; and ordinarily a god is an object of worship before he ever becomes a character in a tale: it is the god's role and actions in a tale that are mythical. To call Zeus a mythical person is like calling Charlemagne a mythical person because he is a character in untrue tales (Zeus may not have existed, but men believed that he did and addressed rituals to him).

My definition is in essential agreement with William Bascom's in his recent article, "The Forms of Folklore" (1965:4): "Myths are prose narratives which, in the society in which they are told, are considered to be truthful accounts of what happened in the remote past" (I omit the author's italics). This definition too insists upon story, narrative, and it implies oral transmission. Both definitions clearly refer to the same kinds of tales. But Bascom's words "considered to be truthful accounts" may lead one to transfer a tale of gods' deeds from myth to folktale once the tale is no longer believed.

Bascom also offers definitions of legend and folktale, with which I can agree after some qualification. "Legends are prose narratives which, like myths, are regarded as true by the narrator and his audience, but they are set in a period considered less remote, when the world was much as it is today." Bascom's distinction between remote past for myths and recent past for legends, as he puts it in his tables (1965: 5, 6), may lead to confusion in dealing with Greek, Norse, Indic, and much other mythology, since often in them the past of legend cannot easily be distinguished from the past of some myths (e.g., certain myths of Zeus's amours, complete tales in themselves, with women who became the mothers of heroes like Herakles and Perseus). It may be better to say "early days of the world" for myths, "early days of the nation (or of mankind)" for legends; yet this distinction will not suit all myths (the tales of Zeus's amours are set in the early days of the Greek peoples, and the Norse myth of Ragnarok is set in the future). Bascom defines folktales as "prose narratives which are regarded as fiction." This is an acceptable definition, provided that we do not include myths and legends which are no longer believed.

The merit of Bascom's definitions is that they divide the material in the right way. My own definitions complement his, and clarify them by distinguishing myth from legend according to the nature of the principal characters. Myths I have defined as traditional tales of the deeds of *daimones*. I define legends as traditional tales of the deeds of heroes, men of a distant past. Heroes may be warriors, kings, founders, benefactors, questers, or even robbers and pirates. It matters not whether the legendary hero is a dimly remembered historical person or a faded god or purely imaginary in his inception: in the legend he is a mortal man who was born and who died, although he did superhuman deeds and gods helped him. Folktales are harder to define in terms of characters. We may say, much as Bascom does, that they are traditional tales of imaginary deeds and events (imaginary to the tellers and listeners, as myths and legends are not likely to be). The characters may be any sort of persons: deities, human beings, animals; the main characters are not likely to be persons of myth and legend, although these are not excluded (as, e.g., in "Cupid and Psyche" and the adventures of Odysseus).

In discussing myths, legends, and folktales, we are concerned with only those traditional tales which introduce supernatural characters and events (including talking animals and their deeds), although these may not be the principal characters and events. Those oral tales which do not have such features—apocryphal tales about historical persons, pseudo-history, obscene stories, realistic popular stories—ought to be excluded from the categories of legend and folktale, at any rate when these are studied in association with mythology and religion. The traditional tales of supernatural persons and events—myths, legends, and folktales, as we have defined them—are in fact associated in tradition, although in some societies distinctions are made between classes of tales with respect to tellers and occasions when they may be told (the Trobriand Islanders have three terms which correspond closely to *myth, legend,* and *folktale* as defined here [Malinowski 1926:24–36]). From ancient Greece they have come down to us undifferentiated as mythology: Apollodoros, Ovid, and Hyginus make no distinctions among what they call *mythoi* or *fabulae*. And *mythology* may as well remain the term that covers all traditional tales of supernatural content. For any particular tale without respect to classification, I suggest the Latin term *fabula*. A recurring pattern or type of fabula we may call a *mythologem*. Since the same plots and themes appear among myths, legends, and folktales, anthropologists and folklorists in the field have often found distinctions hard to draw, as Bascom says (1957:114). These three kinds of fabula, however, are not precisely the same thing; there are external differences of function and internal differences of principal roles (gods in myth, heroes in legend) and often of setting (cosmic or otherwordly in myth, national or local in legend, imaginary in folktale); but some tales are in-between in these respects.[7]

Those who want to efface distinctions between myths and religious beliefs will (and do) combat the suggested definition of myth and mythology. But obviously we have different referents here. The stories are concrete, particular, personal, eventful; gods, spirits, men, animals, do and suffer specific acts at specific times in specific places. Beliefs or creeds are usually stated in general and abstract terms: "Gods rule the world," "Zeus sends storms," "a horsehair put in a tub of water will turn into a snake." These statements are not mythical unless one can prove that they are derived from story contents, i.e., that they are myth fragments or elements (one source of confusion is the equation "mythical = untrue"). Of course, there is some overlap. Some beliefs do have their origin in myths and are expressed in concrete terms: the Apostles' Creed comes to mind (if I may call some of its contents mythical) as a statement of religious belief which embodies narrative statement—yet even here one must notice the tendency of creed to generalize and universalize.

So when I question the theory that all myths have a ritual origin, I mean that I am questioning a ritual origin of all traditional tales; and I am not questioning the statement that ritual formulae, religious creeds, and superstitions have a ritual origin, which is another matter and fairly self-evident for the formulae and creeds. If we are not to distinguish the traditional narratives as *myths,* then we need another term for them.

My definition of myth implies nothing about origins of myth. The fact is that we have no idea how myths began. It is probable that the beginnings of myth are involved with the beginnings of story-telling, and that may have something to do with the origins of speech. Speech is much more likely to have begun in work rhythms (of which the earliest rituals were probably imitations) than in

---

[7] Bascom adopts "prose narratives" for traditional tales. His term is satisfactory, provided that we understand that it intends traditional narratives. And it must not lead us to exclude the narrative conveyed in a folksong or folk poem. In few cases, I believe, is the story invented with the song; the tale has already circulated in prose form. But sometimes the only remaining source of a tale is a song or poem; and the form of the document should not prevent our classifying the tale as myth, legend, or folktale. Bascom's criterion of belief for myths and legends raises problems, since in classical Greece and Italy not everyone who told and heard myths (e.g., Pindar, Plato, and Ovid) believed them to be true. Legends were more universally accepted as the early history of the nation; and many present-day Greeks still believe in their historical truth (e.g., Trojan War legends), excepting perhaps miraculous events. But for all belief in myths and legends one must ask what kind of belief: is it like belief in the Apostles' Creed or like belief in an historical or scientific statement which one receives from authority? I find unsatisfactory the use of "sacred tales" for myths as distinguished from other traditional tales (e.g., Malinowski 1926: 36; Bascom 1965: 5, 6). The term is misleading, since it implies that a people's myths are endowed with sanctity and form a sacred canon. This is true among some peoples, as apparently among Trobrianders, but it is certainly not true of Greeks, Romans, Indians, and many others. The mere presence of gods in tales does not make them "sacred," as it does for C. Scott Littleton, whose article, "A Two-Dimensional Scheme for the Classification of Narratives" (*JAF* 78. 21–27), immediately follows Bascom 1965; the main fault of Littleton's scheme is that a legend must be at least 25 per cent "factual," and may be 75 per cent so. How one should score in the two dimensions, fabulous-factual and sacred-secular, is a very subjective factor too. As for literary critics' use of "myth" (myth is all the rage in current literary criticism), it is often so vague as to be useless, and often enough I have difficulty in understanding just what they mean. Probably Sorel's *Reflections sur la violence* is the fountainhead of the use of *myth* in the meaning "large controlling images" and the like. It may be useful to show what images and symbols have in common with myths, but I believe that no useful purpose is served by confusing them.

rituals.[8] There is little reason to suppose that the earliest language, in our sense of the term, whatever its origins, was not used as language is used today, primarily as a means of communication. This means, as I have already pointed out, that the earliest speakers of real language informed one another about events; these events included exciting adventures, battles, hunting trips, and the like. These were true narratives, initially at any rate. At some point men began telling imaginary tales, either modelled on true narratives or elaborations of true narratives. Into such tales, which we may call folktales and legends, they introduced whatever they were familiar with or believed in. If they believed in ghosts and demons (perhaps true gods were not yet), then ghosts and demons were likely to become characters in their stories. Such tales, if they persisted in tradition (and such tales do persist in tradition without being ritual-bound), were the first fabulae, which in turn produced the first mythologems.[9] This hypothesis about the origin and early development of story-telling does not mean that all myths have an origin in actual events of the dim past, or that every single myth must be traced back to some person's tale of an actual event. It is not an Euhemeristic hypothesis. I do not mean that mythical persons were once real persons: they may be wholly imaginary in their inception. Once myths and folktales became current they obviously suggested other stories framed on similar patterns; furthermore, if legends became myths and heroes became gods, the reverse has happened too: myths have become legends and gods have become heroes. In traditional tales we find recurring types and motifs, a phenomenon which means both that a new story is made on an old pattern, and that a creative story-teller introduces innovations and produces new types.

FUNCTIONS OF MYTH

More fruitful than the subject of myth origins, which we really cannot get at, is that of the functions of myth in a myth-telling society. I agree with most scholars that myths are not explanatory tales devised to satisfy intellectual curiosity. Most of them simply do not explain, and it is only late in history and in a fairly advanced civilization that someone like Hesiod or the compiler of Genesis will consciously use myth as a means of explaining the world. Were early men curious about how the world began, or did they simply take it for granted? Only in advanced societies do we find intellectual curiosity as a force of some power, and in these societies myth is a minor element. We may say that myths have social power in inverse ratio to the amount of intellectual curiosity present in a society. Sounder, I believe, is Malinowski's conclusion (1926:35–59) that myth has a justifying or validating rather than explanatory function: a myth narrates the primeval event which set the precedent for an institution. It may be a ritual institution or cult;

[8] See Karl Bücher, *Arbeit und Rhythmus*, 6th ed. (Leipzig: Reinicke, 1924), especially pp. 245–248; George Thomson, *Studies in Ancient Greek Society* I: *The Prehistoric Aegean* (London: Lawrence & Wishart, 1949), pp. 438–451.
[9] That men in primitive or illiterate societies do inform one another about unusual and exciting events, and that these narratives persist in tradition (as Raglan and Hyman deny), is amply demonstrated by tribal lore gathered from native informants. See e.g., W. S. Nye, *Bad Medicine and Good: Tales of the Kiowas* (Norman: University of Oklahoma Press, 1962) for native accounts of actual adventures which are realistic and lack supernatural and miraculous features; some are verifiable. See Fontenrose 1961:124.

it may be a social, political, or economic institution; it may be a natural "institution," a process or phenomenon important to a society's economy. This is not the same thing as saying that the myths are explanatory, which implies that their sole function is to answer questions about origins. *¹¹*

Whatever the origin of myth-telling, whatever its purpose, myths acquire an ideological character: they often provide a rationale for institutions and customs.¹⁰ Beliefs and creeds serve the same purpose. In advanced societies ideology tends to take the expository form of belief statements rather than the narrative form of myth, although beliefs were surely not absent from the earliest societies. When institutions change, myths and beliefs change; new justifications are needed, and rival parties and factions produce conflicting myths and beliefs. Sir Edward Grey, Governor-General of New Zealand around 1850, may have been the first man to perceive this function of myth. Maori chiefs came to him on questions of war and peace, to present tribal grievances, and to enter into treaties. Later, he said:

> To my surprise, . . . I found that these chiefs, either in their speeches to me, or in their letters, frequently quoted, in explanation of their views and intentions, fragments of ancient poems or proverbs, or made allusions which rested on an ancient system of mythology; . . . it was clear that the most important parts of their communications were embodied in these figurative forms, . . .¹¹

This has been true all around the world. In recent times African tribes have modified their myths to suit institutional changes.¹² This is equally true of ancient Greek mythology: the Theseus legend was transformed under the Athenian democracy. The forms that old myths and legends take in Athenian tragedy reflect fifth-century political events and movements, as several scholars have shown.¹³ Aeschylus' *Eumenides* introduced the episode of trial in Athens into the Orestes legend for the purpose of justifying the recent limitation of the Areopagus court's jurisdiction to cases of homicide.¹⁴ Entirely new myths may appear in a time of revolutionary change, although they usually appear anonymously in a guise of

---

¹⁰ I do not think that the word *rationale* must imply explanation or an attempt to explain: it may imply validation, justification, or precedent. We may notice that throughout history ideologies justify rather than explain.

¹¹ George Grey, *Polynesian Mythology and Ancient Traditional History of the New Zealanders* (London, 1855), preface.

¹² See John Middleton, *Lugbara Religion* (Oxford University Press, 1960), pp. 232–238, 264–270, on the relation of Lugbara mythology to socio-political changes. Interesting is an item in the *Daily Californian* (February 24, 1964): Wolfram Eberhard, Professor of Sociology at the University of California, Berkeley, told a group at the University YWCA that the Chinese Communists are turning traditional Chinese tales to the uses of their propaganda.

¹³ George Thomson, *Aeschylus and Athens*, 2d ed. (London: Lawrence & Wishart, 1946), pp. 231, 276–297; Alan Little, *Myth and Society in Attic Drama* (New York: Columbia University Press, 1942), pp. 7–9, 33, 37–42; T. B. L. Webster, *Political Interpretations in Greek Literature* (Manchester University Press, 1948), pp. 35–40.

¹⁴ I hesitate to say that Aeschylus invented the (legendary) episode of Orestes' trial before the Areopagus court; yet, if I am right about the episode's introduction at this time, it had to arise between 462 and 458. A myth or legend can, in fact, change overnight, and the new form at once presents itself as ancient tradition, nobody knowing where it came from. The Odyssey (3.307) had already connected Orestes with Athens: since he had been in Athens before he killed his mother, why should he not go back to Athens for trial and acquittal? There was also an Orestes in Athenian folklore; see my *The Cult and Myth of Pyrros at Delphi*, University of California Publications in Classical Archaeology, Vol. 4, No. 3 (Berkeley and Los Angeles: University of California Press, 1960), p. 231. In these traditions lay the foundations of the Areopagus episode. It was not the only myth that arose to validate the court's curtailed jurisdiction: another was the tale of the trial of Ares for the murder of Halirrhothios (Apollod. 3. 14. 2).

hoary antiquity. What are the "myths" of Plato but a conscious and deliberate use of this function of myth? They are the fictions of a known author, not traditional tales, and so not genuine myths, as we have defined the term; but Plato had a reason for calling them *mythoi,* or rather (since that is just the Greek word for stories) for making them a political device of his ideal commonwealth (and, indeed, a protreptic device of his philosophy). The Republic will discard the old myths which degraded the gods and will adopt new myths in their place; the threefold division of the citizen body, for example, will be validated with a "myth."

In pointing out this socio-political function of myth I am not saying that this is the sole function of myth; it is not therefore part of my definition of myth. Nor am I saying anything about myth origins. We must not confuse a definition of myth or the functions of myth with the question of myth origins.

Myths, as I have defined them, are stories; and why should all stories have a single origin? And of just what would one seek a single origin? Of that structure which we call plot? Must we look only (or at all) to rituals for that, and not to human speech communicating a sequence of events? Or would one seek a single origin for the contents and themes of myth: the divine and human characters and the miraculous happenings? The ritualists do not make clear what they mean. Raglan says "that to suppose that similar myths [and for him all myths are similar] may have dissimilar origins seems to me like supposing that apples might grow equally well on fig trees," and Hyman has borrowed this analogy.[15] This argument assumes that a myth is the same kind of thing as an apple, and that we can as easily agree upon the referent. The word "apple" has a clear botanical and horticultural definition, and with this denotative meaning nobody confuses figurative uses of the word (as "the apple of my eye"). It is part of the definition of an apple that it comes from an apple tree (also clearly defined). But "myth" is plainly another sort of word. It refers to no visible, tangible object; as we have noticed, speakers and writers employ it in several meanings. Raglan and Hyman take no account of these variable meanings of "myth," and accept all of them as if they were really one thing; looking for a myth tree on which myths grow, they find it in rituals. It is they who try to pick several kinds of fruit from a single tree. We look at their tree and find ritual speeches upon it—prayers and the like. They tell us that these speeches ripen into mythological tales, but never demonstrate the process.

There has been too much theorizing and too little research in the contemporary ritualist camp. We need more analytic study of myths, legends, and folktales, to determine recurring themes and types, and this not in a vacuum, but in their institutional settings. We must also study the stories historically when we can, tracing paths of diffusion and the precise relations, if any, to historical events; for in the instances of Thomas Becket, Guy Fawkes, Charlemagne, and Attila we see that legends have some connection with historical events and at the same time embody traditional themes. We must study the processes by which myths become legends and folktales, gods become heroes, princes, and fairies. And, *vice versa,* we must study how legends become myths, and heroes or kings become gods. We

---

[15] Raglan, note in *JAF* 70 (1957) 173; Hyman 1962a: 276 note.

must study actual associations of myths and rites. Studies of these sorts have been made, and we need a great many more before final judgment can be passed on the ritualist hypothesis.[16]

---

[16] Some valuable recent studies—besides those of Fenton, Laski, and Spencer (see notes 2–4 above)—are Greenway 1964; C. M. Bowra, *Primitive Song* (London: Weidenfeld & Nicolson, 1962), ch. 9; Melville Jacobs, *The Content and Style of an Oral Literature: Clackamas Chinook Myths and Tales* (Chicago University Press, 1959). An interesting book, Adolf E. Jensen's *Myth and Cult among Primitive Peoples* (University of Chicago Press, 1963), translated from his *Mythos und Kult bei Naturvölkern* (Wiesbaden: Steiner, 1951), has recently come to my attention. In this book we have come full circle: myths are first and give rise to cult and rituals; at least myths have primacy, although Jensen appears to say that they are associated with rituals almost *ab initio*. But Jensen includes all religious belief in myth and his book has much more to do with classification of supernatural beings than with tales. His distinction between genuine myths and origin myths (pp. 64–76) is dubious and subjective; he grants that "They belong to the same type of narration" (p. 74), and speaks of a "continuum."

APPENDIX

APPENDIX

THE PALAIKASTRO HYMN

BIBLIOGRAPHY. R. C. Bosanquet, "The Palaikastro Hymn of the Kouretes," *Annual of the British School at Athens,* XV (1908–9), 339–356 and plate XX. Gilbert Murray, "The Hymn of the Kouretes," *ibid.,* 357–365. Jane Harrison, "The Kouretes and Zeus Kouros: A Study in Pre-Historic Sociology," *ibid.,* 308–338. Jane Harrison 1927:1–29. Ulrich von Wilamowitz-Moellendorf, *Griechische Verskunst* (Berlin: Weidmann, 1921), 499–502. Margherita Guarducci 1939: 1–22. M. P. Nilsson 1950:546–550. R. F. Willetts 1962:211–214.

TEXT. *Annual of the British School at Athens* XV, 342–347 and plate XX (Bosanquet); *ibid.,* 357–358 (Murray); Harrison 1927:7–8; Wilamowitz, *Griechische Verskunst,* 499; *Anthologia Lyrica Graeca* II, 279–281 (E. Diehl); Guarducci 1939:7–8; *Inscriptiones Creticae* 3. 2. 2 (Guarducci).

Two copies of the hymn were inscribed on a stele found in 1904 at Palaikastro, Crete, in the course of excavations conducted by the British School at Athens. Three fragments of the stele remain; more than half has disappeared. The date of the inscription is A.D. 200 or later. The following text is a composite of both copies.

PALAIKASTRO HYMN

'Ιὼ μέγιστε κοῦρε, χαῖρέ μοι, Κρόνειε,
πανκρατὲς γάνους, βέβακες δαιμόνων ἀγώμενος.
Δίκταν ἐς ἐνιαυτὸν ἔρπε καὶ γέγαθι μολπᾷ,
τάν τοι κρέκομεν πακτίσι μείξαντες ἅμ' αὐλοῖσιν
5   καὶ στάντες ἀείδομεν τεὸν ἀμφὶ βωμὸν εὐερκῆ.
          ἰὼ μέγι[στε] κοῦρε,   . . .   μολπᾷ.   (6-8)
ἔνθα γάρ σε παῖδ' ἄμβροτον ἀσπί[δεσσι Κούρητες]
10   πὰρ 'Ρέας λαβόντες πόδα κ[υκλῶντες ἀπέκρυψαν.]
          [ἰὼ μέγιστε κοῦρε,   . . .   μολπᾷ.]   (11-13)
     [- - - - - - - - - - - - - - - - - -]
15   [- - - - - - - - - - - τὰ]ς καλᾶς 'Αō̄ς.
          [ἰὼ μέγιστε κοῦρε,]   . . .   μολπᾷ.   (16-18)
     [῟Ωραι δὲ β]ρύον κατῆτος καὶ βροτὸς Δίκα κατῆχε
20   [καὶ πάντα δι]ῆπε ζῶ' ἁ φίλολβος Εἰρήνα.
          [ἰὼ μέγιστε κοῦρε,]   . . .   μολπᾷ.   (21-23)
ἀ[λλὰ βῶν θόρ' ἐς ποί]μνια καὶ θόρ' εὔποκ' ἐ[ς πώεα]
25   [κὲς λάι]α καρπῶν θόρε κὲς τελεσ[φόρος οἴκος.]
          ἰὼ μέγιστε κοῦρε,   . . .   μολπᾷ.   (26-28)
     [θόρε κὲς] πόληας ἁμῶν, θόρε κὲς ποντοφόρος νᾶας,
30   θόρε κὲς ν[έος πο]λείτας, θόρε κὲς Θέμιν κλ[ηνάν.]
          [ἰὼ μέγιστε] κοῦρε,   . . .   μολπᾷ.   (31-33)

Apparatus.   B = Bosanquet.   D = Diehl.   G = Guarducci.

             H = Harrison.   M = Murray.   W = Wilamowitz.

             I = face I of stele (better copy).   II = face II of stele.

1 κῶρε W   Κρόνιε MH   2 γάνος em. W   3 (8, 18, 23, 28, 33) μολπᾶ I   (8, 18, 33)
μολπάν II   7 πανκρα[τὲς γάνους βέβακες]   8 ἐνι[αυτὸν ἔρπ]ε   9 text of G: ἀσπί[δεσσι
Κώρητες] WD: ἀσπι[δηφόροι τροφῆες (Κούρητες B)] BMH   10 κ[υκλῶντες] WDG
κ[ρούοντες] BMH   11–13 missing   14 missing (15 syllables)   15-first 10 syllables missing   ἀῶς W   16 [. . . χαῖρέ μοι K]ρόνειε   17 γάν[ους βέβακες δαιμόνω]ν
18 ἐνι[αυτὸν ἔρπε κα]ὶ εἰς II   19 restored BM   20 [καὶ πάντα δι]ῆπε WDG:
[πάντα τ' ἄγρι' ἄμφε]πε BMH   21 missing   22 γάν[ους βέβακες δαιμόνων ἀγώ]μενος
23 εἰς II   ἐ[νιαυτὸν ἔρπε καὶ γέ]γαθι   24 restored W (DG): ἇ[μιν θόρε κὲς στα]μνία
. . . ἐ[ς ποίμνια] BMH   25 (29, 30) κῆς W   25 [λήι]α BMH   τελεσ[φόρος οἶκος]
WDG: τελεσ[φόρους σίμβλους (ἀγούς B)] BMH: [. . . ὥρας] conjecture M   26 Κρ[όνειε]
27 [δαιμό]νων   28 [ἐνιαυτὸν]   29 ποντο(π)όρος G   30 ν[έους] BMH   κλ[ηνάν] WDG:
κ[αλάν] BMH: κλ[ειτάν] B   32 βέβακ[ες δαιμόνων ἀγώ]μενος   33 ἐνι[αυτὸν ἔρπε καὶ
γέγαθι]

TRANSLATION

Ho, mighty son of Kronos, lord of brightness, hail, thou art ruler of gods.

(4) Come to Dikte at the (new) year and rejoice in song, which we sound for thee to tune of harps and flutes and sing, standing about thy fenced altar.

Ho, mighty son of Kronos, etc.

(9) For here [Kouretes] received thee, an immortal child, from Rea and [with encircling step concealed thee with] shields.

Ho, mighty son of Kronos, etc.

(14) . . . . of the beautiful Dawn.

Ho, mighty son of Kronos, etc.

(19) [And the Seasons] teemed yearly, and Justice held sway over mortal men, [and] prosperous Peace ruled [all creatures].

Ho, mighty son of Kronos, etc.

(24) [But leap (come rushing) to herds] of cattle, and leap to fleecy [flocks, and] leap [to fields] of grain and houses blessed with increase.

Ho, mighty son of Kronos, etc.

(29) [And leap to] our cities, and leap to seafaring ships, and leap to [young] citizens, and leap to renowned Themis.

Ho, mighty son of Kronos, etc.

BIBLIOGRAPHY

BIBLIOGRAPHY

A list of the books and articles referred to in text and notes by author's surname and publication year.

ABBOTT, EDWIN A.
  1898. *St. Thomas of Canterbury: His Death and Miracles.* 2 vols.; London.
ALTHEIM, FRANZ
  1930. *Griechische Götter im alten Rom.* In Religionsgeschichtliche Versuche und Vorarbeiten XXII, 1. Giessen: Töpelmann.
BASCOM, WILLIAM
  1957. "The Myth-Ritual Theory," *JAF* 70: 103–114.
  1965. "The Forms of Folklore: Prose Narratives," *JAF* 78: 3–20.
CONWAY, R. S.
  1928. *The Vergilian Age.* Cambridge, Mass.: Harvard University Press.
EVANS-PRITCHARD, E. E.
  1948. *The Divine Kingship of the Shilluk of the Nilotic Sudan.* Cambridge University Press.
FONTENROSE, JOSEPH
  1959. *Python: A Study of Delphic Myth and Its Origins.* Berkeley and Los Angeles: University of California Press.
  1961. "Some Observations on Hyman's Review of *Python*," *Carleton Miscellany* II, 3: 122–125.
  1962. Review of Hyman, *The Tangled Bank. Carleton Miscellany* III, 4: 73–78.
FORTES, M., and E. E. EVANS-PRITCHARD, editors
  1940. *African Political Systems.* Oxford University Press.
FRAZER, JAMES GEORGE
  1911a. *The Magic Art (The Golden Bough* I). 2 vols.; 3d ed.; London: Macmillan.
  1911b. *The Dying God (The Golden Bough* III). London: Macmillan.
GASTER, THEODOR
  1950. *Thespis: Ritual, Myth and Drama in the Ancient Near East.* New York: Schuman.
GORDON, ARTHUR E.
  1934. *The Cults of Aricia.* University of California Publications in Classical Archaeology, Vol. 2, No. 1. Berkeley: University of California Press.
GREENWAY, JOHN
  1964. *Literature among the Primitives.* Hatboro: Folklore Associates.
GUARDUCCI, MARGHERITA
  1939. "L'inno a Zeus Dicteo," *Studi e Materiali di Storia delle Religioni* XV: 1–22.
HARRISON, JANE
  1927. *Themis: A Study of the Social Origins of Greek Religion.* 2d ed.; Cambridge University Press.
HOCART, A. M.
  1927. *Kingship.* London: Oxford University Press.
  1952. *The Life-Giving Myth and Other Essays.* London: Methuen.
HOOKE, S. H., editor
  1933. *Myth and Ritual.* London: Oxford University Press.
  1935. *The Labyrinth.* London: SPCK; New York: Macmillan.
  1958. *Myth, Ritual, and Kingship.* Oxford University Press.
HYMAN, STANLEY EDGAR
  1948. *The Armed Vision.* New York: Knopf.
  1949. "Myth, Ritual, and Nonsense," *Kenyon Review* XI: 455–475.
  1955. "The Ritual View of Myth and the Mythic." In *Myth: A Symposium,* ed. Thomas Sebeok, pp. 84–94. Philadelphia: American Folklore Society.
  1960. Review of Fontenrose, *Python. Carleton Miscellany* I, 4: 124–127.
  1962a. *The Tangled Bank: Darwin, Marx, Frazer and Freud as Imaginative Writers.* New York: Atheneum.
  1962b. "Leaping for Goodly Themis," *New Leader* XLV, 22 (October 29, 1962): 24–25.

IRSTAM, TOR
   1944. *The King of Ganda: Studies in the Institutions of Sacral Kingship in Africa.* The Ethno-
        graphical Museum of Sweden, Stockholm, n.s. 8. Lund: Ohlsson.
KLUCKHOHN, CLYDE
   1942. "Myths and Rituals: A General Theory," *Harvard Theological Review* XXXV: 45–79.
LANG, ANDREW
   1901. *Magic and Religion.* London, New York, Bombay: Longmans, Green.
MAIR, LUCY
   1962. *Primitive Government.* Baltimore: Penguin Books.
MALINOWSKI, BRONISLAW
   1926. *Myth in Primitive Psychology.* London: Kegan Paul, Trench, Trubner.
MARLOW, A. N.
   1961. "Myth and Ritual in Early Greece," *John Rylands Library Bulletin* XLIII: 373–402.
MEYEROWITZ, EVA L. R.
   1960. *The Divine Kingship in Ghana and Ancient Egypt.* London: Faber.
MORET, ALEXANDRE
   1927. *La mise à mort du dieu en Egypte.* Paris: Geuthner.
MORPURGO, LUCIA
   1903. "Nemus Aricinum," *Monumenti Antichi* XIII: 297–368 and Tables XIV–XVI.
NILSSON, MARTIN P.
   1950. *The Minoan-Mycenaean Religion.* 2d ed.; Lund: Gleerup.
RAGLAN, LORD
   1936. *The Hero: A Study in Tradition, Myth, and Drama.* London: Methuen.
   1949. *The Origins of Religion.* London: Watts.
   1955. "Myth and Ritual." In *Myth: A Symposium,* pp. 76–83 (see Hyman 1955).
RIDGEWAY, WILLIAM
   1910. *The Origin of Tragedy with Special Reference to the Greek Tragedians.* Cambridge Uni-
        versity Press.
   1915. *The Dramas and Dramatic Dances of Non-European Races in Special Reference to the
        Origin of Greek Tragedy.* Cambridge University Press.
ROSE, H. J.
   1959. "The Evidence for Divine Kings in Greece." In *The Sacral Kingship,* Contributions to
        the Central Theme of the VIIIth International Congress for the History of Religions
        (Rome, April, 1955)—*Studies in the History of Religion* IV: 371–378. Leiden: Brill.
SELIGMAN, C. G.
   1932. *Pagan Tribes of the Nilotic Sudan* (with B. Z. Seligman). London: Routledge.
   1934. *Egypt and Negro Africa: A Study in Divine Kingship.* London: Routledge.
WILLETTS, R. F.
   1962. *Cretan Cults and Festivals.* London: Routledge and Kegan Paul.

INDEX

INDEX

Abbott, Edwin A., 16, 18, 69
Aeneas, 36, 37
Aeschylus, 58
Aethiopia, kings of, 10
Africa, killing of kings in, 8–13, 14, 49
African Political Systems, edited by Fortes and Evans-Pritchard, 11
Agamemnon, 8, 15
Aigaion, Cretan mountain, 32
Akitu festival, 5, 7, 24, 50
Aktaion, 53
Alban Hills, 36, 37, 45
Alfred, King, and the cakes, 25 n. 46
Altheim, Franz, 42 n. 10, 69
American Indians, myths and rituals of, 51, 52
Anaitis, Persian goddess, 6
Anna Perenna = Anna, Dido's sister, 46
Antichrist, 20
Apollo, 16, 17; combat with Python, 50
Apollodoros (pseudo-), 30, 55
Apostle's Creed, 56
Areopagus Court, 58
Aricia, chapter iii *passim*
Aristotle, 54
Artemis, 39, 45, 47, 53
Arthur, King, 15
Ashanti, African people, 12
Asiatic Mythology (Hackin and others), 53
Asklepios, 16, 17, 18
Assyria, substitute kings in, 5; sun-disk symbol in, 24
Athens, heroes in, 27, 43, 58
Attila, in legend, 15, 59
Aventine Hill, 40, 42
Avernus, 37

Babylon, festival of Sakaia in, 5, 6; myth of beginnings in, 24; New Year Festival in, 50
Bascom, William, 25, 53, 69; definitions of myth, legend, and folktale, 54, 55, 56 n. 7
Becket, Thomas, 20, 23, 59; cult and legend of, 15–19
Bel, 7
Bengal, kings in, 14
Bergson, Henri, 27
Berosos, *Babyloniaca* 5, 6
Bona Dea = Fauna, 46
Bosanquet, R. C., 63, 65
Brandon, S. G. F., 24
Bristol, celebration of Guy Fawkes Day in, 19
British School at Athens, 29, 63
Brutus, Junius, 48
Brutus Pera, 48

Calicut, kings of, 13
Caligula, Emperor, 39, 40, 41
Cambridge school of mythologists, 1, 26
Canterbury, scene of Becket's martyrdom, 15–19 *passim*
Carmentis, 46

Cato the Censor, 46
Chaka, Zulu king, 11
chantways, Navaho, 52
Charlemagne, in legend, 15, 54, 59
Chaucer, Geoffrey, *Canterbury Tales*, 16
Chesterton, G. K., *The Napoleon of Notting Hill*, 34
Christ story, 18, 52
Claudian gens, 47
Clausus, 46, 47
Colosseros, Aesius Proculus, 39, 40
combat for succession, 9, 24, 36–44 *passim*, 48, 49
Condolence Council of Iroquois, 51
Conway, R. S., 37, 42, 69
Cornford, Francis, 1, 26
Cook, A. B., 1, 26; *Zeus*, 8
Crete, land of Zeus's birth, 29, 33; cult of Zeus in, 29, 32, 33, 63, 66
Cumae, 37
Cupid and Psyche, 55

Dahomeans, kings of, 12
daimones, 32, 54, 55, 57
Darwin, Charles, *Origin of Species*, 34
dead, cult of, 46, 47, 48
Deedes, C. N., quoted, 4
Deganawideh, 51
demonology, 54
Diana, Nemorensis, chapter iii *passim*; Tauric, 42; D.-Vesta, 44, 45, 47, 48; cult in Rome, 40, 42
Dickens, Charles, *Pickwick Papers*, 28 n. 6
Diehl, E., 29, 63, 65
Dika = Justice, 29
Dikte, Cretan mountain, 29, 30, 32, 33, 66
Dinka, king-killing among, 10
Dionysos, 18, 27, 33
Divine King, 1, 8, 59; sacrifice of, 2–4, 8, 10, 11, 14, 20–24 *passim*, 26, 28, 36, 49
Dos Santos, Portuguese traveler, quoted, 10
drama, origins of, 22, 23–25; Athenian tragedy, 23, 27, 34, 50, 58; Shakespearean, 35
dramatic rituals, 23–25, 50–52
Durkheim, Emile, 27, 28, 31

Egeria, 44, 45–47, 48
Egerian gens, 46, 48, 49
Egerius Baebius (Laevius), Manius, 46
Egypt, divine king in, 4, 8, 10, 15; Sed festival in, 7; dramatic rituals in, 23, 24, 50; sun-disk symbol of, 24
Eirena = Peace, 29
Elean women, hymn of, 33
England, cult of St. Thomas of Canterbury in, 17; celebration of Guy Fawkes Day, 19
Eniautos Daimōn (Year Spirit), Harrison's hypothesis of, 27, 28, 34
Enuma elish, 24, 50
Ergamenes, king of Aethiopia, 10

INDEX OF GREEK AND LATIN CITATIONS